TERRORISM
AND THE
ECONOMY

TERRORISM AND THE ECONOMY

How the War on Terror Is Bankrupting the World

Loretta Napoleoni

Seven Stories Press

NEW YORK

Seven Stories Press
140 Watts Street
New York, NY 10013
www.sevenstories.com

In Canada: Publishers Group Canada, 559 College Street, Suite 402, Toronto, ON M6G 1A9

In the UK: Turnaround Publisher Services Ltd., Unit 3, Olympia Trading Estate, Coburg Road, Wood Green, London N22 6TZ

In Australia: Palgrave Macmillan, 15–19 Claremont Street, South Yarra, VIC 3141

College professors may order examination copies of Seven Stories Press titles for a free six-month trial period. To order, visit www.sevenstories.com/textbook or send a fax on school letterhead to (212) 226-1411.

Book design by Jon Gilbert

Library of Congress Cataloging-in-Publication Data

Napoleoni, Loretta.
 Terrorism and the economy : how the war on terror is bankrupting the world / Loretta Napoleoni.
    p. cm.
 ISBN 978-1-58322-895-1 (pbk.)
  1. Terrorism—Economic aspects. 2. Terrorism—Finance.
 3. War on Terrorism, 2001—Economic aspects. I. Title.
  HV6432.N36 2009
  330.9—dc22

                                        2009034062

Printed in the United States of America

9 8 7 6 5 4 3 2 1

To my children

CONTENTS

Acknowledgments ix

Preface xi

Introduction: The Warrior's Folly 1

PART I: SCARED TO DEBT

1. Dubai: The Rise of Islamic Finance 11

2. The Money Trail: Islamic Finance in the Bahamas 21

3. The War on Terror: America's Suicidal Mission 31

4. The Reversal of the Crusades 41

5. Bleeding America Bankrupt: Bin Laden
   Fulfills His Dream 57

6. The USA PATRIOT Act: A Self-Inflicted Wound 73

7. Oil as a Retaliatory Weapon 83

8. Scenes from the Global House of Cards 93

PART 2: THE FALL OF THE GLOBAL
HOUSE OF CARDS

9.   The Bubble Bursts   105

10. The Politics of Fear   109

11. Las Vegas and Dubai: "Mirror, Mirror,
    on the Wall, Who's the Richest of Them All?"   121

12. The Danger of Protectionism   135

13. A New Economic Model   141

Bibliographic Notes   153

Index   159

ACKNOWLEDGMENTS

This being the first book I have written originally in Italian after many years, I must confess that it was a most rewarding experience to work again in my mother tongue. I thank Lorenzo Fazio, director of Chiarelettere, who in the aftermath of the collapse of Lehman Brothers suggested that I write it, and Luigi Bernabo, my Italian agent, who convinced me to accept Chiarelettere's offer.

I sat down to work and, by reordering my thoughts and rereading some of my articles and speeches, came to understand so many things that I might never have while commenting daily on the financial crisis. Sometimes one needs to have the time and the courage to reread what one has written in the past to better focus on what is happening in the present.

We are in the throes of a sort of "perfect storm," resulting from a confluence of financial abuse and political negligence. Although this idea emerges from many of my articles, it has not been easy to focus on the conceptual while in the midst of the biggest economic crisis of the postwar period. Discussing this book with my American publisher Dan Simon, my editor Ria Julien, and my American agent Diana Finch helped me enormously to avoid the distraction of everyday events and to maintain a long-term perspective.

My guardian angel, Claudia Segre, who works in the financial markets, has been, as always, a precious friend and provider of data, statistics, and commentary, offering a profound vision of this financial earthquake and gracious company during a most valuable week in the United Arab Emirates.

My journalist colleagues at the periodicals for which I write regularly—*Internazionale, l'Unita, il Caffè, Mondo e Missione, El País, Vanity Fair Spain, Vanity Fair Italy*, and numerous others—likewise have been fundamental in helping me understand what is not working in global finance.

Sincere thanks go to my friends Laura Paganin and Tonino Giuffrè, who hosted Claudia and me in Bahrain, and to Marco Masulli who served as our interpreter. Thanks as well to Stephen Creaturo and Clare Chalmers for their input on the world financial situation, so too to Cristina Masazza, who assists me in all my labors. I also thank Antonio Zoppetti, who maintains my Italian blog, for having dealt so well with my delays in responding to the requests of readers due to the demands of writing. And thanks to the readers, who write in daily with questions, ideas, and suggestions; without them this book surely would have been sterile, devoid of "real" stories.

My husband and my children, as always, have been a great support and have put up with yet another Christmas spent with documents, statistics, and pages strewn around the house.

PREFACE

Toward the end of 2009, newspaper headlines told us that the recession was over. World leaders complimented each other for having avoided another great depression. Goldman Sachs's and J. P. Morgan's exceptional profits in the third quarter of the year apparently had triggered the euphoria, yet unemployment kept rising in the United States and in the rest of the world. Economists explained that the world was likely in the midst of a recovery, though it did not command a rise in employment. Most people had difficulty in grasping such a concept. "How can we be out of the woods if more and more people are still getting lost inside them?" they asked.

On the terrorism front, the news seemed even less optimistic. The US and its allies found themselves bogged down in Afghanistan, and people perceived the exit strategy for Iraq as weak and faraway on the horizon. Pakistan became a big worry. The birth of new armed organizations, among them the Pakistani Taliban—a group that many believe is funded by the Taliban, Gulf states, and even rogue elements from India—troubled Washington and the world. The Pakistani Taliban pursues identical goals to those of Mullah Omar's followers: they want to destabilize Pakistan to set up their own Islamic state. Spreading from Waziristan, the tribal belt area where

Osama bin Laden and Ayman al-Zawahiri took refuge after the Battle of Tora Bora, they aim to become an active force all over the country.

A buoyant trade in heroin, for which production rose 400 times since the US invasion, bankrolled the Taliban. The organization no longer depended on handouts from Gulf donors and Pakistan's Inter-Services Intelligence (ISI), but achieved a steady income by reinventing themselves as narco-warriors. Under the nose of coalition troops and inside a country that America's military intervention transformed into a democracy, this rugged army of religious fanatics succeeded in keeping the strongest and most modern military machine in the world under check, thanks to the explosion of the narcotics trade. It seems absurd that with coalition forces on the ground, poppy production has risen. But this is exactly what has happened. Even more surreal is the fact that such military intervention is the root cause of the astonishing debt accumulated by Washington and of the credit crunch.

But the failures of the Afghanistan "mission" go well beyond the military humiliation. The Western-style democracy that Washington exported at the expense of a historically gigantic debt have proven to be a farce. President Hamid Karzai was reelected thanks to bribes and fraud, yet nobody can do anything to stop the charade, a degeneration of the democratic ideals of the founding fathers. The political situation in Afghanistan is a stalemate, both militarily and politically, and the United States has no control over it.

In Iraq, Washington faces a similar ordeal. Corruption and sectarian hatred block all attempts to make inroads into a true democracy. Terrorism has not been defeated and US troops will most likely have to prolong their presence in the country well beyond President Barack Obama's term in office.

One cannot avoid pondering an uncomfortable question: Was it worth bankrupting America and forcing the world into a serious recession in order to export Western-style democracy to countries that do not even understand its true meaning? Was it worth risking the consequences of such a decision, consequences that are likely shaping a new world order, a world in which the US no longer holds a position of unique power but shares its leadership with other emerging countries such as China?

Watching Washington and Beijing interact on the world stage means watching the balance of power shift eastward. At the end of 2009, President Obama visited Asia, not as the most powerful man on Earth but as the leader of a country that is losing two wars, is crippled by the economic crisis, and sees unemployment rising above 10 percent. The US finds itself a "leader," who has imposed protectionist measures against its banker China to boost the domestic economy, tariffs that have not triggered a single retaliation from Beijing; China needs America less and less, to the point where US protectionism does not affect it!

Instead, America needs China today more than ever. Barack Obama is the president of a country that, since 9/11, has financed its folly with the savings of Chinese workers, a nation that still relies upon the Chinese to underwrite its mounting debt—at least that is what the average Asian thinks. It is from a position of weakness that America now attempts to emerge as a winner after a decade of madness. Will it succeed at untangling the many knots it has created between terrorism and the economy? A timid attempt has been made to close Guantanamo, put an end to the concept of terrorism as war, and bring this despicable phenomenon back into the boundaries of criminality. But the road ahead is full of obstacles.

At the end of 2009, the decision to bring Khalid Sheikh Mohammed and a few of his accomplices to trial in New York for the 9/11 bombing split American public opinion. Many people feared the presence of high-ranking al-Qaeda members on American soil; others welcomed the possibility of sentencing them to death for what they did in 2001. This dispute had nothing to do with the Obama administration's policy toward terrorism but sprang from the difficulties in defining acts of terrorism within the boundaries of national laws, both in times of peace and in times of war. Such complexity is intimately linked with George W. Bush's war on terror.

Terrorism is elusive; each time someone believes he or she has found the correct definition, someone else proves it faulty. As a concept, it is hard to pin down because it is essentially a political phenomenon. What is the difference between a freedom fighter and a terrorist? It depends on the angle from which one is looking. To the apartheid South African government, Nelson Mandela was a terrorist; he spent twenty-six years in prison for crimes linked to the use of political violence. Yet most of the world supported the decision of his group, the African National Congress, to use violence to end apartheid. More to the point, today Mandela is the celebrated father of a democratic country: South Africa.

Even the qualifying observation that terrorism's victims are primarily noncombatants fails to isolate the uniqueness of this phenomenon. Since World War I, the number of civilians killed in acts of war has risen, and today they represent by far the highest number of casualties of any armed conflict.

To add to the confusion, after 9/11 the Bush administration launched the war on terror, granting terrorists the status of unlawful combatants, which they never had before, and presenting terrorism as a threat to national security instead of as a menace to law and order. Until 9/11, the judiciary had primarily addressed terrorism: the police persecuted terrorists, who ended up being prosecuted in courts of law. Thus, Ramzi Joseph, the man who masterminded the first World Trade Center bombing, currently is held in a high security prison inside the US. He has not been executed, as his uncle Khalid Sheikh Mohammed, will most likely be because the US introduced the death penalty for acts of terrorism only after 1993. Both approaches, however, recognize the criminal nature of the phenomenon and it is this element that constitutes the core of the concept of terrorism, one universally accepted.

Terrorism poses a unique threat to the modern state. Indeed it triggers a dilemma: How to deal with it? Treat it as a threat to national security, as Bush did? Or as a form of vicious crime, as the European states did during the second half of the twentieth century? To resolve this dilemma, terrorism should be regarded as a crime with war aims—a simple yet useful definition, one that can be applied to any form of terrorism. The Irish Republican Army (IRA) and the Basque Euskadi Ta Askatasuna (ETA), defined as nationalist armed organizations because they sought territorial independence from the legitimate state, committed crimes that they justified as acts of war. The same principle can be applied to any type of terrorist organization, from al-Qaeda to the Red Brigades, from the Animal Liberation Front to American antiabortion groups.

The core of the definition of terrorism rests, therefore, in a criminal act, and thus the criminal nature of terrorism is its true essence. The political element becomes a motivation. This can easily be extended to transnational terrorism, whereby an attack in one country is launched from a foreign safe haven. This definition does not provide a legal framework for the use of a prison like Guantánamo, which does not have jurisdiction over crimes committed in another country. Thus the Obama administration's decision to use US courts of law to try members of al-Qaeda for crimes committed inside the US proves that even Washington agrees that the criminal component represents the essence of terrorism.

To disentangle terrorism from the economy, one has to disassemble the war on terror. But if closing Guantánamo and bringing to justice the perpetrators of 9/11 are within the Obama administration's reach, ending the wars in Iraq and Afghanistan seems to be a utopian goal. What is bankrupting America is an unwinnable war on two fronts, a war that someone else is funding: China, who buys US debt. Is America going to face the same problems that confronted the other cold war superpower—the USSR—in Iraq and Afghanistan? More importantly, will these wars end the US's superpower status?

On the twentieth anniversary of the fall of the Berlin Wall, it is now the US that is losing a war in Afghanistan, a war not unlike the one that indirectly contributed to the breakup of the USSR. Where coalition forces today battle the Taliban and al-Qaeda, the Soviets in the 1980s fought the *mujahideen*, a Muslim army of volunteers that Moscow called terrorists. The anti-Soviet *jihad*, a brutal war funded by the US Central Intelligence Agency (CIA) and the Saudis, became too costly for Moscow, almost bankrupting the Soviet state. In a painful and humiliating withdrawal, the last Soviet troops left Afghanistan in February 1989, just a few months before the implosion of the Soviet system. Without that defeat, we might not be celebrating the twentieth anniversary of the end of the cold war or a unified Europe today. Remarkably, the central Asian country of Afghanistan seems once again to be shaping our future.

It is paradoxical that the graveyard of one superpower should become a battlefield for the other. It is even more ironic that the United States, the very nation that used the mujahideen and this deeply hostile country to defeat the Soviet Union, should now have fallen victim to its own ordeal on the same terrain. The similarities between the two Afghan wars are countless. The Soviet generals kept requesting more men in order to gain control of this vast land because its high-tech war machinery did not work against such evasive enemies. The US and coalition armies face the same problem: mainstream war tactics do not deliver the expected results. All victories turn out to be illusions. As the Soviet generals found out, securing a village is pointless because the day after, the terrorists are back in control of its streets. The Taliban are as elusive as the mujahideen; they vanish into the hills at night and are back fighting in the morning. Both groups riddled the main roads with hidden explosives—the mujahideen used antitank mines while the Taliban employ improvised explosive devices, homemade bombs—to blow up soldiers on patrol as well as civilians.

Even the geography of the wars is remarkably similar with much of the fighting during the anti-Soviet jihad taking place in the south, near the Pakistani border. The mujahideen took refuge from the Soviet army in Waziristan, where today the Taliban and al-Qaeda have their headquarters. Most Soviet soldiers who died lost their lives in Kandahar and the Helmand province, the troubled areas of this new Afghan war.

Perhaps the most remarkable similarity between the two wars resides in their final objective: to transform Afghanistan into a friendly country by turning its political status into a replica of the invading superpower's. Twenty years ago, Moscow wanted Afganistan to become a satellite state of the Soviet Bloc; today the US wants to turn it into a Western-style democracy. This is a dangerous exercise in nation building.

Until the fall of the Berlin Wall, the US had been cautious in playing this game, which seemed to be more of a Moscow pastime. Two of Washington's prior attempts—turning defeated World War II enemies Germany and Japan into democratic countries—had been successful, even if it was only with the reunification of Germany fifty years later that the US finally completed its job. The fall of the Berlin Wall showed that democracy was transferable and that it was a remarkable force for bringing nations in line with the American vision of the world. Perhaps watching Europeans tear apart the wall with their bare hands in order to reach friends and relatives across that cold-war divide had convinced the US that democracy was the most powerful weapon it possessed. That might explain why, after the end of the cold war, nation building became Washington's preferred pastime.

A 2003 RAND Corporation study shows that of the fifty-five peace operations mounted by the US since 1945, forty-one came after 1989. Police intervention has always been followed by nation building, and the record seems very poor: In 1993, Washington pulled out of Somalia at the first sign of resistance. In 1994, it opted to let an international force restore order in Rwanda. It hesitated before joining European troops in Bosnia and before committing itself to a military intervention in Kosovo. But each time it went in, the "US-led intervention has been wider in scope and more ambitious than its predecessor," concludes the report.

George W. Bush criticized Bill Clinton's attempts to spread Western democracy, but after 9/11 he ordered a massively ambitious nation-building plan for Afghanistan and Iraq. None of the post–cold war presidents, including Barack Obama today, have understood that nation building is not primarily about economic reconstruction but rather about political transformation. Americans are making the same mistakes the Soviets did. The US has failed to install viable democracies in Somalia, Haiti, and Afghanistan because all three countries are divided ethnically, socioeconomically, or tribally. In Afghanistan, Western-style democracy may well be the wrong model to apply.

The Soviet Union crumbled when the economic and political model upon which it rested became obsolete; the Kremlin failed to modernize and the ill-fated war in Afghanistan exposed this failure. Moscow should never have gotten involved. Now Washington risks the same level of failure if it limits its modernization merely to the election of Barack Obama, the first black president, who campaigned on the promise of change. What is needed is a fresh, new approach to bringing peace and prosperity to countries fundamentally different from our own.

The war on terror has nothing to do with defeating al-Qaeda. Rather, it has represented the *casus belli* needed to launch into an ambitious and phenomenally expensive nation-building project. To fund such folly, Washington did not hesitate to bankrupt the country and trigger the biggest credit crunch in modern history. President Obama endorsed the bailout and refrained from redesigning regulation, which has a lot to do with the wars in Iraq and Afghanistan. Washington needs Wall Street's help to keep international investors funding the US debt, which in turn provides the $1.6 billion needed each month to keep troops in Iraq and Afghanistan. The president and his administration are trapped inside a vicious cycle and nobody has the strength to break it, as that would require declaring defeat on two fronts. The American people are held in a vise: fearing terrorism and bankrolling a reckless financial system. Terrorism seems to have won this first round of confrontation, a sad conclusion for the free world.

THE WARRIOR'S FOLLY

Terrorism and the economy: the two most discussed topics of the last few years. But what if their relationship went well beyond sharing the front-page headlines? What if the war on terror, launched by George W. Bush in the aftermath of September 11, 2001, contributed to the credit crunch and to the global recession? These are some of the uncomfortable questions we will attempt to answer.

When President George W. Bush took office in 2000, his administration inherited a small budget surplus, but he hardly returned the favor to his successor. President Barack Obama, taking office in the midst of the worst economic crisis of the postwar period, faces a national debt of $10 trillion—about 70 percent of the country's gross domestic product (GDP) or 18 percent of the world economy. Where did all this money go in the span of eight years? Two wars, still underway, and an extremely ambitious—albeit inconsistent and inefficient—security system have drained American finances and pushed the United States into the ranks of the nations with the highest public debt.

This scenario would have been inconceivable twenty years ago when fiscal revenues, rather than low interest-rate policies, funded America's wars. How can we forget Lyndon Johnson's historic decision to increase taxation to meet the escalating cost of the Vietnam War? This was a necessary and, at the same time, profoundly unpopular choice. After all, few want to finance the military machine with their own money, even if the objective is to destroy a super-terrorist like Osama bin Laden or to rid the world of an arch-dictator like Saddam Hussein. Nonetheless, some critics wonder why the unpopular wars in Iraq and Afghanistan have not generated a social movement as strong as the one that forced Washington to end the Vietnam War.

One reason is thus: until military expenses affect our pockets or limit our liberty—in other words, unless we're forced to fight—conflicts remain virtual, experienced exclusively through the filter of the media. Not even the terrorist attacks in Madrid and London, both linked to the Iraq war, sufficiently brought that conflict home in the West to motivate people on either shore of the Atlantic to get involved in ending it. The threat of terrorism only touches us intermittently, when the images of blood and death fill our television screens or when politicians use them to scare us. After the attack in Mumbai in November 2008, the Italian foreign minister declared that terrorism, not the recession, threatened the world. For days, Italian newspapers and TV news programs stressed this message, reminding the public of their seven compatriots trapped inside the terrorist-occupied hotels. Italy fell victim to its fear of Islamic fundamentalists to the extent that two Moroccan simpletons ended up being mistaken for al-Qaeda's super-terrorists. The reasons for the accusations appeared even more ridiculous: that both men inculcated in their two-year-old children the cult of Osama bin Laden—a man whom they called "uncle"—and both dreamed of blowing up a suburban convenience store, without possessing any explosives, arms, or ammunition.

The fear of terrorism has been an extremely effective instrument used to distract Western citizens from the economic chaos of the last twenty years, and the threat of future attacks temporarily diverted people's attention from the proceeding credit crunch, an economic cataclysm that triggered a world recession, one possibly as serious as the Great Depression. Sadly, the link between terrorism and the economy is not entirely one of diversion. The war on terror, the brainchild of American neoconservatives, has indeed contributed to the current economic crisis. It has hurt our pockets, reduced our financial prospects, mortgaged the future of our children, and impoverished Western living standards. We simply do not realize the full extent of it.

The seeds of the credit crunch were sown twenty years ago when the fall of the Berlin Wall marked the beginning of the politics of cheap and easy credit denoted by a steady fall in interest rates. Alan Greenspan, at the helm of the Federal Reserve, became the master of the new credit society. His deflationary policy smoothed globalization, or, better put, eased Western finance's colonization of the world economy. The state withdrew from the economic arena and left the task of managing the economy to the financial markets. It's no wonder that in the 1990s Alan Greenspan became more powerful than President Bill Clinton. Greenspan controlled the functioning of the world economy and orchestrated its seemingly unstoppable growth. Each time an economic crisis tested the new system—from the collapse of the ruble to the US mini-recession of 2000—Greenspan lowered interest rates and postponed the crisis. This was strategic folly because, far from resolving the structural economic problems linked to globalization, deflation delayed and eventually magnified the impact of the crisis.

At the same time, ordinary citizens lost control of politics as they participated less and less in the running of the state. The policy of lower taxation, which marked the administrations of Clinton and of both Bushes, reduced taxpayers' level of interest in the management of state funds. The years of economic bonanza, mortgaged on the back of easy, cheap credit, facilitated public disinterest in the state's financial strategies. The euphoria of these decades distracted taxpayers from the erosion of one of the cornerstones of the social contract: the state must justify to its citizens how it spends their money. As the state became less fiscally transparent, the public became less vigilant.

After 2001, the policy of low interest rates became a necessity for the US government, which, in the space of two years, found itself embroiled in two wars. These conflicts promised to be brief and easy, but today they continue to weigh heavily on the national budget. The administration avoided raising taxes, instead increasing the national debt by selling treasury bonds internationally. But gathering money on the international capital market presents problems. The Treasury must compete with the private sector so the Bush administration pressured the Federal Reserve to prolong the policy of low interest rates. Cutting interest rates increases the competitiveness of treasury bonds vis-à-vis those issued by the private sector and by other governments. It raises the yield, the return on the invested capital.

Soon China and Japan, followed by several Arab oil-producing countries, became the largest clients of the US Treasury, de facto funding the bulk of America's debt. After 9/11, an aggressive policy of low interest rates, one that eventually led to the credit crunch, became imperative to bankroll two wars.

The deflationary policy, therefore, first financed the illusory growth of globalization and subsequently funded the war on terror. If during the 1990s Greenspan created the bubble, after 9/11 the financing of two conflicts inflated it. The practice of maintaining low interest rates after 2001 produced the perverse mechanism of subprime mortgages. This inflated property prices, and from 2001 to 2007 they climbed as never before. This phenomenon, in turn, kick-started the borrow-to-invest spiral—the securitization of the debt, in bankers' jargon—and eventually led to bank failures and the credit crunch.

Now Americans are paying the price for this economic folly. Taxpayers, who have been kept in the dark for fifteen years about the functioning of a globalized economy—people who were unaware that Beijing, Tokyo, and Riyadh funded Bush's wars—are finally experiencing a reality check. The social contract, despite being eroded, is still in place and, in the final analysis, those who have to answer for the debts of the state are those who constitute it: the citizens. Americans are already shouldering the burden of the credit crunch. To save the financial system and fund two wars, Washington is using both present and future taxpayer money, to the tune of over $3 trillion. As Americans mortgage the wealth of future generations, they seem twice victim to the poor management of the state.

Just as US taxpayers are taking this bitter medicine, the taxpayers of the global village cannot escape the consequences of Greenspan's deflationary folly. The United States is the world's economic locomotive, and when the economic crash occurred in the fall of 2008, the conflagration on Wall Street dragged the entire planet into recession. Then, when Americans battled the recession with protectionist measures and rhetoric, the entire world followed suit. Once again the ghost of protectionism threatens to strangle international trade and transform a serious recession into another Great Depression.

Is it possible that the destruction of the twin towers of the World Trade Center—witnessed live around the world—set off a chain reaction of such magnitude as to cripple the world's strongest economy and to readjust the economic equilibrium of the global village to the detriment of the United States?

Today, America is less economically potent than it was a decade ago. Many believe that the era of its economic supremacy is coming to an end and that when the world reemerges from the great recession, the locomotive will have moved east to China, with the epicenter of world finance found in the shadows of minarets: Islamic finance, embryonic until 9/11, is today the most dynamic financial sector in the world, displaying the highest rate of growth. Will Barack Obama succeed in altering this trend?

Paradoxically, many of these changes appear to fulfill Osama bin Laden's great dream of destroying the American economy and resuscitating the Islamic empire, the caliphate. In 1998, after having been exiled from his native Saudi Arabia and from his adoptive Sudan, bin Laden launched his anti-Zionist, anti-American campaign, identifying in the distant enemy (America and its Western allies) the root causes of the problems of the Arab and Muslim worlds. The objective was to weaken the American economy to the point of forcing Washington to abandon its policy of support for the oligarchic Muslim regimes, Saudi Arabia being the leading one. Only then would the jihadist revolution have free reign in the Muslim world.

Naturally this plan was a fantasy that existed only in the imagination of al-Qaeda, as was the entire jihadist movement. Before 9/11 few knew of its existence, and those who believed in it did so irrationally as an act of faith. In the span of a mere eight years, bin Laden's dream is about to become reality. But it was not the Prophet who made it happen nor al-Qaedism, the anti-imperialist movement born from the ashes of al-Qaeda after the destruction of the Taliban regime. It was the unexpected by-product of the folly of the war on terror—the credit crunch—that brought Western economies to their knees.

Nobody is innocent. Even we, unconcerned citizens of the neoliberal state, bear some responsibility. In exchange for ever-lower taxes, easy credit, cheap products, and good markets, Westerners let bankers such as Greenspan and politicians like Bush and British Prime Minister Tony Blair fool us with impunity. We are, paradoxically, also the victims of our own ingenuousness because we allowed ourselves to be cowed by the propaganda of fear. We should have sensed that a band of religious fanatics did not have the power to destroy Western capitalism. But those at its helm, the "Masters of the Universe" and the Wall Street scions—they did.

The genesis of the credit crunch and global recession, which today threaten the very existence of the capitalist system and of our daily lives within that system, rests in the decisions taken in the aftermath of 9/11 and in the unwillingness of Western citizens to confront a political elite no longer at our service.

If we really want to get out of this crisis, a recession that also affects the soul of the global village, we must have the strength to confront our mistakes and become engaged in politics. We may need to renew the political class, possibly not once but many times, until we are satisfied with those who represent us. The United States of America is attempting to do so, and Great Britain is following suit. History will tell if they will succeed.

In order to succeed, this revolution needs to take place, first of all, in our minds. The current credit crunch and our present economic hardships teach us that citizens should not let politicians lie, and that when this happens it is our right and duty to rebel. While the politicians scared us with the threat of al-Qaeda, Wall Street stole our savings. Now the money is gone, and we are being asked to save the robbers. If we want to prevent another similar crisis, we must have the strength to say no and to turn our backs on the great illusionists of our time: the politicians, who until today have so badly represented us.

PART 1

SCARED TO DEBT

CHAPTER 1

DUBAI: THE RISE OF ISLAMIC FINANCE

Dubai sits at the heart of the Muslim world. On the eastern shores of the Arabian Peninsula lies the latest casualty of the credit crunch, another shooting star that fell to earth just a year after Lehman Brothers. Broke, abandoned by the jet-setters who vacationed on its sandy beaches and reprimanded by Abu Dhabi, its more conservative, oil-rich neighbor who refused to bail it out, Dubai's downfall symbolizes the decadence and danger of emulating the West.

Among the Arab emirates and the Islamic countries, once Dubai ranked as the most successful at bridging two worlds, Islam and the West, a process through which it lost its true identity and assumed a new one that fit beautifully with the nouveaux riches who flocked to its shores. Dubai epitomized the globalized metropolis of our world, a place as shallow as its sandy beaches and as fictitious as its man-made islands. Today, the sad story of its bankruptcy, which ended the construction of the highest skyscraper in the world, once again fills our newspapers. But few people understand that the genesis of this modern Babylon runs parallel with that of the credit crunch. In a perverse twist of destiny, right from the beginning Dubai was caught in the web of deceit that Washington created to convince us of the absolute necessity of the war on terror. It is in Dubai that our story starts. . . .

A bridge between the Middle East and Asia, it is a one-hour flight from Karachi and two hours from Kandahar, the former capital of the Taliban regime. In the days leading up to the fall of the Taliban regime in 2001, word had it that airplanes stuffed with banknotes and gold bullion shuttled to and from Dubai, depositing such fortunes in anonymous checking accounts and safe deposit boxes.

Based on these reports, observers have wrongly accused this emirate's Islamic banks of doing business with al-Qaeda and the Taliban. Prior to 9/11, despite its status as an important tax haven, the bulk of Dubai's banks mirrored Western credit institutions. All that would change after 9/11, thanks to the USA PATRIOT Act. Although the first Islamic bank, Dubai Islamic Bank, opened its doors in 1975, for decades Islamic banking remained embryonic across the Muslim world.

The metamorphosis of this city into an Islamic financial metropolis began at the end of 2001, when Dubai emerged as one of the global village's financial hubs in the midst of tough post-9/11 antiterrorism monetary controls. A popular vacation destination of globalization's superrich, who frequent its sunny beaches during the winter months, Dubai soon became the Monte Carlo of the Middle East, a place to enjoy one's wealth away from fiscal and monetary controls. Celebrities bought houses on the extravagant man-made islands scattered along its coastline, sandbars shaped by imaginative architects, and inlayed with resorts and trophy homes. A shrine to the unlimited power of money to even redesign the ocean's coastline, Palm Jumeirah, the artificial island shaped like a palm tree and constructed in 2001, is perhaps the most famous of all.

Dubai and 9/11 are deeply intertwined, and their relation-ship goes well beyond the obvious fact that part of the money that paid for the destruction of the twin towers passed through the emirate's banking system. This Arab emirate is an impor-tant tax haven, a place where money transits freely from control or regulation. Offshore facilities resemble impenetrable webs, and, indeed, to this day nobody has managed to discover who sent the money to Mohamed Atta and his accomplices. The Dubai–9/11 relationship also encompasses the role played by the emirate and other Muslim countries in the globalized economy. Though it may sound implausible, as soon as the West focused its attention on the war on terror, the United Arab Emirates and the rest of the Persian Gulf began experi-encing an unprecedented economic boom. Money started to flow toward their economies.

Those who moved to Dubai in the 1990s attest to the trans-formation of a city that, until twenty years ago, was a small, insignificant village closed around an old port from where pearl fishermen departed daily. Pearl trading represented the only commercial activity of the Arab emirates prior to the discovery of oil. Lacking significant oil reserves, Dubai decided to become a financial hub for its oil-rich neighbors. In the 1980s, oil pro-ducers from Saudi Arabia and other emirates began utilizing its sophisticated and tax-free banking infrastructure. Toward the end of the 1990s, Western financial institutions realized the importance of its strategic position and opened branches in the city. For Arab and Muslim clients, the emirate also came to rep-resent an important access point to globalized finance.

The great leap forward, however, took place in the 2000s. The economic consequences of 9/11, not globalization alone, morphed a small stretch of sand between the desert and the sea into an international metropolis, a new giant rivaling New

York and Tokyo. Bush's war on terror prompted these developments, setting in motion several devastating unforeseen events. Four key factors, all intimately linked to America's response to 9/11, converged and turned this emirate into the Muslim Wall Street: the boom of Islamic finance triggered by the Patriot Act, the emergence of Eastern tax havens, the housing bubble, and the hike in oil prices.

The link between Dubai and terrorism goes well beyond Atta and his accomplices' trip to the capital of vice; it encompasses the way modern finance likes to do business. It seems logical, therefore, to start the investigation of the relationship between terrorism and the credit crunch with Dubai. But to understand the role that this emirate played in the meltdown of Western capitalism, it is imperative to first comprehend the genesis of Islamic finance itself and to investigate the root causes of America's unusual reaction to 9/11, a response that classified al-Qaeda as a threat to national security, an enemy so powerful as to demand not one but two wars.

ISLAMIC FINANCE AND WESTERN CAPITALISM: TWO MODELS OF GROWTH

The notion of an Islamic financial system is as old as Islam itself, dating back to the era of the prophet Mohammed. It springs from the Qur'an's prohibition on charging interest, or *riba*. *Sharia*, the Islamic law, considers riba a form of usury and therefore regards it as unlawful, *haram*. It was only in the mid-1950s, however, that economists, bankers, intellectuals, and Arab scholars began to seriously consider the possibility of creating a financial system without interest rates.

The underlying principle behind the rejection of riba is simple: Money cannot generate money. Money must be used as a productive means to create something tangible. According to this principle, speculation is synonymous with gambling and other unlawful activities. The Islamic economic system also incorporates elements that traditionally have nothing to do with finance or economics but represent the fundamental tenets of Islam: the *zakat*, the religious almsgiving requiring all Muslims to pay 2.5 percent of annual profits or disposable income, and the *hajj*, the pilgrimage to Mecca.

The first projects of applied Islamic economics had these fundamental principles in mind, taking place in the 1950s in rural Egypt and outside Kuala Lumpur, Malaysia. The Egyptian project in Mit Ghamr was a private initiative to fund the construction of housing for the poor, and the Malaysian initiative used the zakat levied by Islamic financial institutions to fund the hajj for those who could not afford such a journey.

Until the early 1970s, Islamic finance remained embryonic, and people looked upon it with great skepticism, mainly because it lacked capital. But the first oil shock in 1973 and '74 changed this scenario, for oil-rich countries suddenly had the financial means to create the first Islamic banks. They were codesigned by sharia scholars and religious leaders together with Arab oil tycoons and bankers. It was an unusual, yet rock-solid, joint venture.

This marriage between religion and finance is unique in economics, as is the partnership between bankers and clients. This peculiar relationship springs from the concept of the *ummah*: the community of believers, considered the collective identity of Muslims, a body that breathes and prays in unison. The ummah is the beating heart of Islam. Thus, the philosophy upon which the new economic system rests implies a shared risk taken jointly by the bank and its clientele.

Naturally, this principle is foreign to modern capitalism, a system that strives to maximize profits and minimize losses. This happens either by diversifying, transferring, or selling risk. Indeed, at the core of the current credit crisis, we find the commercialization of risk transformed into a valuable commodity. When the risk that binds bankers and clients is sold to a third party, the direct link between the original two parties ceases to exist.

Islamic finance does not accept nor allow this separation. Under this system, money must still produce tangible returns. Though the Qur'an does not permit interest payments, Islamic banks benefit from income generated from rentals, copyrights, earnings from commerce, and the sale of goods. The relationship between the client and the bank resembles a business partnership: the bank funds the purchase of real estate or buys products, commodities, and so on, and the client repays the loans through monthly payments and becomes the full owner.

A committee of religious experts presides over Islamic banks and verifies that every financial transaction conforms to the sharia—is "sharia-compliant," in the jargon of finance. Once satisfied, the board issues a *fatwa*, a religious edict guaranteeing that the bank markets a sharia-compliant product. This unusual structure offers the Islamic banking system infinite flexibility. Potentially, Islamic finance can bankroll any activity, ranging from the financing of real estate loans or infrastructure, to oil exploration, and even athletic sponsorships—providing they are not haram.

The sharia, like all religious laws, rests on universal ethical principles that constitute the boundaries within which Islamic banks can operate. The root causes of the credit crunch lie in the erosion and disappearance of a similar code of ethics in Western finance. In the 1990s, deregulation filled this void. New financial tools, such as derivatives, altered balance sheets and increased banks' leverage instead of protecting producers and consumers from price fluctuations. Paradoxically, this void has not been filled by new regulation; Western powers seem unwilling even to partially reverse deregulation.

Conceptually, Islamic economics is the opposite of capitalism, a system centered on the individual whose engine is capital accumulation. East of Europe, Adam Smith's "invisible hand" does not exist. In the Eastern world, the selfish behavior of each individual, aimed at maximizing profits and minimizing costs, is not believed to miraculously enrich entire nations. In the short shadow of the minarets, wealth comes from cooperation and joint ventures between banks and clients. The strength of this union represents the solid foundation of Islamic banks and, at the same time, the engine of its growth in the Muslim world.

In the second half of the 1970s, Islamic credit institutions multiplied in Egypt, Kuwait, Sudan, Bahrain, and Jordan. In 1979, Pakistan and Iran began converting their banking systems to become fully Islamic. But it was not until the world economy suffered two major crises—the crash of the Asian stock market in 1997 and 9/11—that Islamic finance actually blossomed. The crash created a gap between Muslim investors and modern capitalism, while the attacks on the twin towers prompted a clear break. This alternative form of finance represented—and continues to represent—Islam's collective answer to the failures of Adam Smith's invisible hand. Thus, Islamic finance seemed to have grasped capitalism's flaws and foresaw the credit crunch a decade before it happened.

In the late 1990s, Malaysia pioneered the new Islamic economic model. At the height of the Asian market crisis, then Malaysian Prime Minister Mahathir bin Mohamad rejected the intervention of the International Monetary Fund (IMF) in his country. He criticized Western speculation for devaluing Asian currencies and accused Western finance of purposefully weakening the economy of his country. In what was an unexpected move to many, he converted the Malaysian financial system into a sharia-compliant alternative, kick-starting the process of "Islamization" of the banks.

Bin Mohamad turned to his Muslim brethren in the Gulf for help, to secure their financial support and attract their capital through the sale of sharia-compliant products. *Sukuk*, Islamic treasury bonds, were featured at the top of the list. Thus the first Islamic financial rescue package became indisputably a great success.

THE POST-9/11 BOOM IN ISLAMIC FINANCE

By the time al-Qaeda destroyed the World Trade Center, Malaysia had developed a sophisticated and fully operative banking system. In the wake of 9/11, many investors rushed to "Islamize" their portfolios, and a large chunk of these funds ended up in Malaysia and Dubai. As we shall see in Chapter 6, more and more Arab investors withdrew their investments from the West, fearing the Patriot Act, visa restrictions, and the freezing of Muslim accounts. They began acquiring Islamic financial products, and Malaysia and Dubai had many to offer.

From that moment, the Islamic financial market boomed. While the West focused on the symbolic and verbal clashes between East and West, theorized by Samuel Huntington in his "clash of civilizations" thesis, the movers and shakers of global finance turned eastward and forged lucrative alliances with the Muslim world.

The crisis of 9/11 offered Islamic finance a much-awaited opportunity to attract a critical mass of capital required for the infant industry to take off. From the end of 2001 until 2006, the value of Islamic shares traded on the secondary market increased from nearly zero to $45 billion. According to Moody's rating agency, at the end of 2004, Malaysia issued $41 billion of sukuk, about 75 percent of all Islamic shares. The Gulf countries followed suit with $11 billion more.

From 9/11 onward, Islamic finance grew exponentially, becoming an integral part of the global village. In 2003, the first sukuk issued in dollars appeared on the Eurobond market; in 2004, the German state of Saxony issued sukuk for €10 million; in 2004, the first European Islamic bank, the Islamic Bank of Britain, opened for business; in 2006, a group of European and Arab investors laid the foundation for the European Islamic Investment Bank. In June 2006, Deutsche Bank decided to issue a sukuk bond loan of about $500 million for the Islamic Development Bank, based in Jeddah, Saudi Arabia.

Eventually, Western banks and financial institutions understood the potential of this new financial sector. In turn, they started to woo a select group of Islamic scholars, offering them lavish compensation in exchange for creating Islamic finance sectors and issuing fatwas for all sorts of sharia-compliant financial products. For example, starting June 2006, Lloyds TSB began offering Islamic financial services at all its national branches.

At the end of 2008, it was estimated that global investment in Islamic finance amounted to $2,000 billion, with a growth rate of 15 percent. But that was not all. More than 400 institutions operated in this market and managed investment funds for about $70 billion. Institutional bonds amounted to $6 billion. Islamic finance proved to be the most dynamic sector of global finance. Before the credit crunch, its size and volume were expected to reach 10 percent of the world's economy by the end of 2009.

The ascendance of Islamic finance illustrates the blithe indifference of Western governments to an emerging system that would pose a challenge to Western economic hegemony. As this new landscape emerged, the war on terror created a climate of fear that enveloped the West, blinding leaders to the economic challenger in their midst and citizens to their leaders' looting of the Treasury. At the same time, Islamic finance offered many rich Muslims the same advantages and opportunities of traditional Western finance.

In the 1990s, together with Islamic finance, tax havens and offshore banks had begun to take shape in the Muslim world. Prohibition of riba and respect for the principle of partnership did not clash with the institution of offshore facilities. Dubai became one of these networks' most important hubs, explaining why the money received by Mohamed Atta in the US came from this emirate. Yet in the aftermath of the attack, nobody followed the money trail, which soon went cold. Why not?

CHAPTER 2

THE MONEY TRAIL: ISLAMIC FINANCE IN THE BAHAMAS

After 9/11, the world had a unique opportunity to understand Islamic offshore facilities, a web of banks and financial hubs where dirty and terror money freely moved around—or at least this is what many terrorist experts believed about offshore banking. The complex financial empire of Bank al-Taqwa, an Islamic offshore giant registered in the Bahamas, could have offered us a unique view into a sector of international finance still unknown. But we never had the chance to gain this valuable insight because the investigation into its finances turned into an embarrassing fiasco.

Understanding the structure and purpose of al-Taqwa, regardless of its alleged role with Muslim armed organizations, would have helped us comprehend the functioning of offshore Islamic banks and shed some light on their ties with jihadist groups and organized crime. Such knowledge could have proven invaluable for avoiding mistakes not only in the war on terror but also in the fight against organized crime, which uses Islamic tax havens to launder money. Finally, an in-depth understanding of Islamic offshore facilities could have been of service in combating tax evasion and fiscal fraud, two issues today at the center of Western politicians' battle to raise money to offset the ballooning public debt.

In 2001, people knew very little about the Islamic financial system and even less about the tax havens emerging at its center. Many analysts admitted to being deeply skeptical about the impact of these tax havens on global finance, yet nobody could have denied the ties between Dubai and the Taliban regime or the role of the anonymous Dubai accounts from which money had been sent to Atta and his accomplices. Unfortunately, this vague assessment of an unknown financial world—a world regarded with a mixture of indifference and arrogance—also tainted the behavior of US financial investigators. As a consequence, the trail that led to Bank al-Taqwa went cold.

Deep down, however, the US had no interest in following the money trail. In the aftermath of 9/11, the world was in the grip of mass hysteria, and unsubstantiated accusations were sufficient to blacklist both individuals and companies. Propaganda alone was enough to make everybody believe that Washington's objective was to cut the terrorist lifeline: money. In reality, the main goals of Bush's war on terror did not include the destruction of al-Qaeda's finances. Bush seized the opportunity presented by 9/11 to launch and implement a hegemonic plan to pursue a new foreign policy agenda, one that the neocons had crafted during the Clinton years. The president and his cronies neglected to analyze the ties between terrorism, crime, and Islamic finance because they considered them irrelevant and secondary to their real goal.

The fiasco that resulted from investigating Bank al-Taqwa proves that countering terrorism finances came a distant third to reestablishing America's hegemony in key areas of the world and to proselytizing the neocon hegemonic creed. The failure to investigate seems particularly relevant because it took place precisely at the moment Washington sold the war on terror to the American taxpayer as an absolute priority, one that justified economic sacrifices and limitations to personal freedom. One can now can say that the fiasco of the al-Taqwa investigation contributes to proving Washington's well-hidden, true intentions.

BANK AL-TAQWA, A MISSED OPPORTUNITY

Even today, countering terrorist financing is given very low priority. Against this background, many question the effectiveness of increased airport security, which submits travelers to humiliating and tedious rituals before boarding a plane, while the money that will finance the next devastating terrorist attack continues to freely circulate around the world. Such measures do not protect us. The simple truth is that they are mere window dressing, and the way the investigation of al-Taqwa was conducted confirms it.

In November 2001, while a fragmented al-Qaeda ran away from the final push by coalition forces into Tora Bora, the United States approached the United Nations and requested that Bank al-Taqwa Ltd. be put on the terrorist sponsors list. The bank is an institution with a very peculiar profile: an Islamic offshore bank incorporated in Nassau, Bahamas, with subsidiaries in Liechtenstein and a management branch in Lugano, Switzerland. The request came as no surprise. For years, the bank had been under the magnifying glass of financial investigations in several countries, yet no formal charges had ever been formulated.

The bank was founded with capital of $50 million by six wealthy Arabs in 1988. They had ambitious plans and opened a subsidiary bank in Liechtenstein and a management branch in Lugano, Switzerland, soon after. The brain behind al-Taqwa was Youssef Nada, an Egyptian with an Italian passport. Considered a financial maverick, Nada was well known to US financial investigators who had investigated several of his companies after Black Tuesday in 1987. However, the authorities could not prove any irregularities.

During the 1990s, Nada and his financial partners used al-Taqwa to conduct their businesses without breaking any official rules. The bank grew and attracted new shareholders and investors. In a good year, it managed about $220 million—not a small amount for an institution of its size. In 1995, the Italian antiterrorist agency Division for General Investigations and Special Operations (DIGOS) began investigating the Lugano branch in relation to alleged financial contributions to the Islamic Cultural Institute in Milan.

The DIGOS investigation focused on the charitable work of Ahmed Idris Nasreddin, the founder of the bank and then member of the board of directors. Ethiopian-born Nasreddin had worked for the Binladen Group, a Saudi construction company, and was the honorary consul of Kuwait in Milan. He also acted as a board member of the Islamic Cultural Center of Milan and chaired the Islamic Community of Ticino. Allegedly, DIGOS feared that Nasreddin's charity had altered the amount of humanitarian funds sent to Bosnia and that the funds exceeded what had been raised.

In Germany, the authorities conducted a similar investigation. The object this time was the work of another partner of Nada's, Ali Ghaleb Himmat, who, like Nada, resided in Campione, Switzerland. He chaired the Islamic Center in Munich, a key magnet for Muslims in the country. Founded in 1928 in Egypt, this center hosted many Islamic religious groups.

BEFORE 9/11

In 1997, DIGOS finally issued a formal report, but only after *Il Corriere della Sera*, a prominent Italian daily, had run an investigative article on Bank al-Taqwa's alleged link with Middle Eastern extremist groups. In the report, DIGOS admitted that the bank was under investigation for an alleged transfer of $60 million to the military faction of Hamas and to other Middle Eastern fundamentalist groups. Again, no proof for such accusations could be found.

The management of al-Taqwa denied any wrongdoing and challenged *Il Corriere della Sera* with a lawsuit. It was at that point that the Swiss authorities began an inquiry into the al-Taqwa branch in Lugano.

"Toward the end of 2000, the Swiss Federal Bank supervisors and the Federal money-laundering police conducted a review of the bank," recounts Rico Carisch, who investigated the bank's finances for the UN. "On its own initiative, the bank hired PricewaterhouseCoopers for an audit. No suspicious activities were found. Still, the Swiss requested a review of the group's headquarters in the Bahamas. In reaction to that, on April 12th of 2001, the Bahamian Central Bank revoked the banking license of Bank al-Taqwa Ltd. on the basis that it would no longer tolerate shell banks." However, nobody communicated this decision to the Swiss or to any other European authorities, nor did the al-Taqwa principals reveal to the Swiss authorities that their Bahamian license had been revoked. Without the license, they could no longer justify the existence of the al-Taqwa management branch in Switzerland, which had always maintained that it acted only as a service and management subsidiary of the principal Bahamian bank.

Unaware of the closure of the Nassau bank, the Swiss

authorities issued an administrative order for a name change of al-Taqwa Management to Nada Management, to avoid confusion between the two banks. "From Switzerland, Nada Management continued its activities through the intricate financial web it had created during the previous decade. Money raised in the Gulf reached Switzerland and Great Britain. The European tax haven route simply replaced the Bahamanian one. A sophisticated system of Chinese boxes spread across several countries hid the origins and destination of the transactions," concluded Carisch.

As pointed out by a US Treasury official, at their origin these funds were always "clean," coming from donations, deposits, investments, and the zakat. In the 1990s, the bank passed reviews and inquiries related to money laundering and the illegal transfer of funds with flying colors. The real problem was how these funds were used once they reached their destination, but nobody bothered to raise this point. "Far from paying attention to this detail, all authorities in charge of investigations concentrated on the origin of the funds, ignoring the ultimate beneficiaries," adds Carisch. "The lack of cooperation between the Swiss and Nassau financial authorities, due, in essence, to the secrecy that prevails in fiscal havens, made it impossible to trace the money and even allowed the bank to continue to operate after the license of the main bank had been revoked."

Against this background, al-Taqwa escaped the first round of investigation in the US. When President Bush signed Executive Order 13224 on September 23, 2001, authorizing aggressive action against bankers with ties to international terrorism, he did not mention Bank al-Taqwa. The US came into this knowledge a week later when an investigative journalist, who for obvious reasons wants to remain anonymous, handed the list of al-Taqwa's shareholders to the US authorities. US investigators then obtained from the Bahamas the bank's registration papers and a nineteen-page document listing ordinary shareholders, preferred shareholders, and redeemable shareholders, totaling hundreds of names from various countries. Among them stood two members of the bin Laden clan.

According to *Salon*: "Included on the list [were also] Yousuf Abdullah Al-Qaradawi, the grand mufti of the United Arab Emirates, and five members of his family; Mariam Al-Sheikh A. Bin Aziz Al-Mubarak of a branch of the Kuwaiti royal family; and members of the prominent Khalifeh family of the United Arab Emirates . . . and Hassan el-Banna, a leader of the Egyptian Moslem Brotherhood group."

THE TERROR LISTS

On November 7, 2001, in an amendment to the executive order, the US blacklisted al-Taqwa, some of its affiliates, and the principal shareholders. Days later, the UN Security Council released an identical list, but the full list—the one containing the names of all the shareholders—was never handed over to the Security Council.

Let us look more closely at these terror lists and how they function. They contain a directory of physical and legal entities suspected of financing armed groups. People are blacklisted on suspicion, pending an investigation. The aim is to freeze all accounts and prevent evidence attesting to complicity with armed groups from disappearing. Each country has its own list; the UN has the most comprehensive one, but it resembles the photocopy of the American terror list. To date, there is no protocol to compare the names on the various lists.

The actual way in which US authorities implicated al-Taqwa

should make us reflect on the usefulness of such lists. The cited evidence was too generic. The announcement by the White House contained only unspecified allegations: "Al Taqwa provides investment advice and cash transfer mechanisms for al Qaida and other radical Islamic groups." During the investigations, aside from the few well-known executives—including Youssef Nada, Ali Ghaleb Himmat, and Ahmed Nasreddin—no other shareholder was interrogated, though others clearly must have been very familiar with the bank's operations.

The only antiterrorist measure taken against al-Taqwa was freezing its assets on both shores of the Atlantic and imposing the UN travel ban on Youssef Nada pending a full investigation. From Switzerland, however, Nada traveled freely to Liechtenstein. In Vaduz, he change the names of al-Taqwa Trade, Property and Industry Company Ltd. and Ba Taqwa for Commerce and Real Estate Company Ltd. to Waldenberg SA and Hocberg SA respectively. He then appointed himself liquidator and put Waldenberg into liquidation.

SECRECY BUT NOT COOPERATION

Naturally, no one in Vaduz knew that Nada had been included on the UN terror lists. Bush fought the war on terror not at the helm of cooperation but under a banner of secrecy. No protocol was created to share information among countries. "By the time the Swiss authorities realized what Nada had done and appointed their own liquidator there was nothing to 'liquidate,'" reveals Carisch.

Secrecy and lack of cooperation also discouraged the Bahamas, Liechtenstein, Switzerland, and Italy, the four countries that investigated al-Taqwa before and after September 11, from cooperating and exchanging their own data. Nada traveled to Vaduz, despite UN-imposed movement restrictions, and liquidated institutions that had been frozen due to alleged connections with the financing of terrorism.

The failure to solve the mysteries of al-Taqwa is intimately intertwined with the real motives of the war on terror, a conflict centered around the military intervention in Iraq, not the destruction of al-Qaeda's finances. This has become a serious problem for everybody.

After 9/11, a new witchhunt began, further hiding the true motives of the war on terror. Thousands of innocent individuals ended up on blacklists, trapped in a financial Guantánamo that is as illegal as the Cuban one is real. Those who bankrolled al-Qaeda disappeared and remain unpunished. To comprehend the magnitude of this operation, consider this: Up until the time of this book's publication in late 2009, only four people mentioned in the lists have been found guilty. Dozens of individuals and companies have been removed from the lists due to lack of evidence, but hundreds of thousands still await pending investigations.

Thus the outcome of the investigation into Islamic offshore banks is depressing: was al-Taqwa guilty of the crimes accused of by the US? We know that it is possible, and in fact very likely, that the bank had absolutely no ties with al-Qaeda, but we cannot prove it. Proving or disproving such an accusation would have shed some light on a financial system that today threatens Western financial supremacy. It also would have helped us understand how money from Dubai reached those nineteen men who brought to America its worst nightmare. Another piece of the 9/11 puzzle is lost forever due to the inefficiency of the system of controls, a smoke screen to the true motivations of the war on terror.

CHAPTER 3

THE WAR ON TERROR: AMERICA'S SUICIDAL MISSION

THE ACCUSATIONS AGAINST BUSH AND BLAIR

The Bush administration's answer to 9/11 was the "war on terror," a unilateral and selfish response that the world not only accepted but embraced. In the aftermath of the tragedy, the Bush administration did not seek the assistance and cooperation of nations that had battled with terrorism for decades. On the contrary, Washington took the lead and completely revolutionized the meaning of terrorism.

Until 9/11, terrorism belonged to the criminal arena. Terrorism was crime with political aims, a serious threat to law and order, not to national security. Therefore, law enforcement and the judiciary, not the military, orchestrated the fight against armed organizations. Bush disregarded these notions and strategies. Preferring to launch a war in faraway lands, he granted al-Qaeda the status of enemy. Behind this arrogance lay the US administration's ulterior motives, goals fundamentally different from those presented to the public and publicized by the media as the protection of American soil.

Clearly, hunting bin Laden's bankers—perhaps the most effective means to neutralize the threat of al-Qaeda—did not represent Washington's top priority, but why?

On September 6, 2003, Michael Meacher, former environmental minister in the Blair administration, answered this question. In an editorial published by the *Guardian*, he accuses Bush and Blair of having done nothing to prevent 9/11. He claims that the tragedy instead offered George W. Bush the much-needed casus belli to launch America's expansionistic, hegemonic policy in the Middle East and in other key areas of the world.

Rebuilding America's Defenses, a policy document published in the summer of 2000 by the Project for the New American Century, a neoconservative think tank, contained the blueprint for Washington's aggressive foreign policy. While the now disgraced clan of Vice President Dick Cheney, Donald Rumsfeld, Paul Wolfowitz, Jeb Bush, and Lewis "Scooter" Libby commissioned the document, *Rebuilding America's Defenses* was primarily the brainchild of Cheney. Back in 1992, he formulated its core message, which can be summarized in one of the sentences of the document: "America needs an aggressive and unilateral approach in foreign policy, one that would secure [US] dominance of world affairs, by force if necessary." The proposed strategies to pursue such an ambitious objective included creating a US military presence in the Middle East to contain and combat Iran; achieving military control of Iraq, with or without Saddam Hussein; maintaining military bases in the Arabian peninsula after a regime change had taken place in Iraq; wresting control of peacekeeping missions from the UN; and discouraging other industrialized nations from taking a leading role in the international community.

Michael Meacher claims that embarking on and implementing such a policy of world domination required the vast popular consent that only a major tragedy, a casus belli, would instantly create. The events of 9/11 offered solid, almost universal backing, Meacher suggests. He also draws a parallel to another defining American tragedy—the attack on Pearl Harbor—suggesting that the advance warning of an imminent attack never reached the US fleet in the Pacific Ocean or was simply ignored. The US, he puts forward, had the opportunity to prevent 9/11 but purposely did not intervene in order to fulfill Washington's plan to launch a global war of domination under the guise of the war on terror.

A SUICIDAL WAR FOR HEGEMONY

These accusations are by no means groundbreaking news. After 9/11, journalists, academics, intellectuals, Federal Bureau of Investigation (FBI) and Central Intelligence Agency (CIA) agents, and other secret service personnel conceded that in the months prior to the attack there was enough intelligence available to predict and prevent it. What makes Meacher's revelations particularly disturbing is the fact that they come from someone who sat in Blair's cabinet on 9/11, the most loyal and important US ally.

Meacher's editorial is not a piece of investigative journalism geared to uncover a conspiracy theory, and indeed one should not see any such theory behind it. He never stated that the US voluntarily let the tragedy unfold. Washington had no prior specific knowledge of the attacks, but had enough information to foresee them and intervene before they occurred. All the government needed to do was piece together the intelligence gathered over several months, an exercise that never took place.

In hindsight, the evidence is astounding. At least eleven coun-tries alerted the US to the possibility of a major terrorist act, among them Algeria and Egypt. In the spring of 2001, Con-doleezza Rice even warned the administration that an attack involving airplanes was in the pipeline. After the meeting, then Attorney General John Ashcroft stopped flying on commercial flights and got clearance to use private jets. In the summer of 2001, two top officials from the Mossad, the Israeli national intelligence agency, traveled to Washington and alerted the FBI and CIA that a terrorist cell of 200 Islamists loyal to bin Laden was preparing a big attack. The officers handed over the list of names, among them four of the nineteen hijackers, who were already living in the US. at that time.

In August 2001, a flying instructor in Minnesota alerted the police that one of his students wanted to learn only how to steer large planes and not how to land. This led to the pre-emptive arrest of Zacarias Moussaoui, the twentieth hijacker. When the local police found out that the French government had a file concerning his links with Islamist terrorist groups, they arrested him and confiscated his laptop, on which they found several clues to the logistics of the 9/11 attacks. "Mous-saoui might have being planning to crash an aircraft into the twin towers," one of the officers wrote in his report.

Many other alarm bells rang before 9/11. In 1999, for exam-ple, the US National Intelligence Council report stated that "al-Qaeda suicide bombers could crash-land an aircraft into the Pentagon, the headquarters of the CIA, or the White House."

But to investigate the links between the credit crunch and the war on terror, it is not crucial to know whether the US could have preempted the attacks and, indeed, chose not to do so.

Another key question seems much more relevant: In the aftermath of the cold war, did Washington grossly underestimate the consequences of globalization, to the extent that it missed the demise of its own power as the world's leader? Did this oversight empower the very forces that today are eroding America's economic supremacy, the new political and economic agents that have emerged during the delicate transition from the bipolar equilibrium of the cold war to the current globalized disorder? Among these, one cannot ignore the rise of Muslim economic and financial power and the advent of the Chinese superpower.

It seems that Bush led America on a suicide mission, setting the country down a path that has ended with its economic decline. He launched a war the nation could not afford either financially or ideologically, and today not only America, but also the entire world, is paying for his decision.

POOR JUDGMENT IN WASHINGTON AND THE GROWTH OF ISLAMIC CAPITAL

Washington's ambiguous relationship with Osama bin Laden well illustrates America's ill judgment about the globalized world and its role in it.

Bin Laden played a key role in the last decade of the cold war. He was an important go-between for the Saudis—who together with the CIA bankrolled the anti-Soviet jihad—and the mujahideen, the Muslim fighters who opposed the Soviets in Afghanistan. When the war ended, bin Laden returned to Saudi Arabia where he received a hero's welcome. It was only in 1991, at the outset of the Gulf War, that his relationship with some members of the Saudi ruling elite began deteriorating. Eventually, incensed by his vocal opposition to the king's decision to let US troops into Saudi Arabia and his accusation that, by doing so, the House of Saud violated the religious sanctity of the country, the Saudis stripped him of his citizenship and issued a warrant for his arrest.

However, nothing was done to bring him to justice. Instead, the royal family let him move to Sudan with a large chunk of his fortune in tow. His role within Saudi society earned him this special treatment and consideration. In the eyes of the Saudi population, bin Laden symbolizes their emancipation from the West. His power, well before 9/11, became iconic and intertwined with the Muslim victory over the Soviet super-power in Afghanistan. Shockingly, in dealing with the threat posed by bin Laden, the US administration ignored these important details.

America did not pay attention to the changes underway in the Muslim world either. In the 1980s and '90s, the emergence of Islamic banks promoted the growth of new social classes composed of bankers, traders, and merchants. After the victory in Afghanistan and the breakup of the Soviet Union, these new social classes began to infiltrate the territories of the former Soviet republics where Muslims lived. This process, which can be described as the Islamic colonization of the Muslim world, is one of globalization's unforeseen side effects, driven by an unusual alliance between the Wahhabi, the ultra-conservative religious militants who maintain intimate ties with armed Islamic groups, and the emerging Islamic middle classes. Osama bin Laden became one of the icons of the Islamic colonization, an emblem of the ongoing Muslim strug-gle to gain independence from the West.

A noble endeavor in the eyes of its supporters, this process of Islamic colonization prompted the funding of mosques and *madrassas* in key regions of the Muslim world, from Albania to Uzbekistan. Throughout the 1990s, within the walls of these religious schools, the indoctrination of a new generation of jihadist warriors took place. Meanwhile, Islamic capital funded armed groups battling pro-Western, corrupt oligarchies from Uzbekistan to Indonesia and those who fought foreign powers, as in Chechnya. In exchange, Muslim businesses penetrated the economy of these countries and built a solid Islamic economic infrastructure.

Western powers remained unaware of, or purposefully ignored, the great changes taking place in the Muslim world. How else can one interpret US indifference vis-à-vis Osama bin Laden's anti-American propaganda and the spreading of radical Islam along the borders of the former Soviet Bloc? How else can one justify the fact that until 9/11 bin Laden traveled freely, and in the summer of 2001 even underwent surgery in a clinic in Dubai?

Paradoxically, prior to 9/11, Washington's so-called Muslim "enemies," not the US administration, actively tried to capture bin Laden and opposed radical Islam. Libyan leader Muammar al-Gaddafi was the first to issue an international warrant for the arrest of the infamous Saudi. In 1998, al-Gaddafi uncovered an al-Qaeda–bankrolled assassination plot masterminded by the al-Muqatila, an Islamist group of former mujahideen who had fought in Afghanistan. According to documents recovered after the fall of Saddam Hussein's regime, the Iraqi dictator also feared the surging jihadist wave that, since the anti-Soviet jihad victory in Afghanistan, had been riding across the Muslim world. Saddam managed to keep it at bay until his fall.

Why did the US not join in the manhunt? The US had good motivation to do so: al-Qaeda had bombed US embassies in Africa and attacked the *USS Cole* in Yemen. The Clinton and Bush administrations even had plenty of opportunities to capture or eliminate bin Laden. In 1996, General Elfatih Erwa, the Sudanese minister of defense, offered to extradite him to

America from Sudan, where he resided at the time. The US authorities declined. When Erwa asked what they should do, the Americans replied, "Let him go wherever he pleases, except for Somalia," where an al-Qaeda cell had been involved in the killing of US soldiers during the peacekeeping operation. As we all know, bin Laden went to Afghanistan.

Even after 9/11, more opportunities to neutralize bin Laden arose. In October 2001, the Pakistani Islamic parties negotiated with the Taliban and with bin Laden to extradite him to Pakistan, where he had agreed to stand trial for 9/11. Once again the Americans declined the offer "on the slight chance that they would capture him." But when, in November 2001, the US Navy had bin Laden and the Taliban leadership in firing range at least ten times, Washington's authorization to proceed did not arrive in time.

Why did the US miss so many opportunities to bring the man who masterminded 9/11 to justice? Before the tragedy, capturing bin Laden would have put the US–Saudi relationship under serious pressure. Worshipped as an Arab hero in Saudi Arabia, bin Laden had maintained strong links with powerful clerics. In a BBC broadcast aired in November 2001, FBI agents admitted that both the Clinton and Bush administrations had not wanted to strain relations with America's most valuable ally in the Middle East by hunting bin Laden, someone who was not regarded as a real threat to America and its foreign policy. This was a gross miscalculation, a strategic error. After 9/11, such mistakes became apparent and yet no major effort to capture or dispense with him took place. The delicate diplomatic ties between Washington and Riyadh continued to condition the Bush administration. In retrospect, not capturing bin Laden deeply wounded America and the world; it was a potentially irreparable strategic miscalculation.

THE CLASH OF CIVILIZATIONS

From the fall of the Berlin Wall until 9/11, indifference to the outside world characterized the US establishment. In the prevailing intellectual climate of *laissez-faire* of the 1990s, the neocon ideology hatched; a decade later it blossomed thanks to the Bush administration's aggressive, bellicose foreign politics. After 9/11, Washington had to confront the changes underway in the world but attempted to do so without fully reckoning with their magnitude. The world had evolved because of the demise of communism and the advent of globalization, two phenomena that truly did not interest the neocons. Since the victory of the cold war, US foreign policy had been in suspended animation, trapped inside that magic moment.

Ultimately, a decade of diplomatic disinterest morphed into the bellicose foreign policy of the Bush administration. It was apparent as early as mid-2003 that this aggressively reactionary policy was backfiring: in Afghanistan and Iraq, civil wars were raging—not at all the expected blitz-war actions, these had turned into difficult and costly conflicts with no end in sight; terrorist activities in the world proliferated; public debt in the US steadily increased. Far from being won, the war on terror continued to weigh heavily on the nation's finances and bin Laden still roamed free.

At that point Washington changed its tune and presented a new scenario. The enemy ceased to be a handful of crazy religious fanatics, "cave dwellers" as Bush loved to repeat. In the summer of 2003, the enemy became a sophisticated international network of banks, charitable organizations, Islamic fundamentalist institutions, and entrepreneurs. The administration had changed their propaganda tune and the media followed suit. Al-Qaeda became an active agent of "the clash of civilizations." Bush's rhetoric of 9/11 applied Huntington's cultural conflict of historic proportions between East and West. But Bush misread the situation. Islamic terrorism had nothing to do with the clash between two cultures. Rather, it resembled a collision of titanic proportions between two economic systems, one hegemonic and the other insurrectional. Yet nobody dared to question Bush's vision, whose popularity at the time was much higher than that of President Obama's on the day he won the US election. The world wanted to believe that the American crusade was going to save it from an imaginary enemy. History would prove the exact opposite.

CHAPTER 4

THE REVERSAL OF THE CRUSADES

WARS OF ECONOMIC LIBERATION

In his speeches, Osama bin Laden has often drawn parallels with the Christian Crusades, accusing Americans of being new crusaders engaged in a colonial war to subjugate the Muslim world. He portrays the Islamist jihad against the West as a justified response to an atavistic aggressor. Paramount to this vision of the contemporary or modern jihad is the nature of the threat: an alien and ruthless enemy defined by religious creed (or lack thereof)—Christianity and Judaism for the Zionist crusaders in the Islamist jihad, communism for the Soviets in the anti-Soviet jihad. Against this backdrop, Islam's current enemies are modern, high-tech replicas of the medieval Frankish knights, the bloodthirsty Christian savages who, at the beginning of the last millennium, brought down its splendid civilization.

In the time of the Crusades, the invasion of the Christian knights triggered a defensive jihad. Centuries after, the practice had been forgotten; at the same time, it helped rediscover the ancient meaning and power of jihad. Stimulated by the ferocity and bellicose ardor of the Franks, Arab warriors rallied around Saladin and eventually repelled the invaders. In the last few decades, Islamist ideologues and armed groups have recalled Saladin's jihad as a triumphant phase in Islamic history and warned of a renewed Christian crusade. Building upon this comparison, radical Arab ideologues, like the Egyptian Islamist Abd al-Salam Faraj, have called for a new jihad. In turn, bin Laden and his associates expanded this concept to justify acts of terrorism against Westerners, including civilians. George W. Bush's aggressive language only reinforced the Islamist analogy with the Crusades. Since 9/11, the rhetoric in Washington under Bush was that of a holy war, a crusade fought not to free the Holy Land in the name of Christ, but waged in defense of humanity under the banner of democracy. Recurrent religious imagery in Bush's speeches, coupled with his doctrine of preemptive strikes, boosted the belief among many Muslims that the war against Iraq was yet another manifestation of American imperialism in the Middle East, another chapter in the new Christian crusades.

Ironically, the motivations, objectives, and organization of the Islamist jihad are very similar to those of the First Crusade (1096). For several centuries, Islam had dominated the Mediterranean Basin, a hegemony that had blocked European economic development and growth. Therefore, the First Crusade was a powerful challenge to the sole superpower of the time, and its success marked the beginning of Europe's climb back to power. As Islam progressively lost its economic grip over the Mediterranean, the Crusades emerged as a critical chapter in the eastward expansion of Europe, a form of medieval imperialism. Christianity provided an ideological umbrella under which a unique coalition of forces gathered to set a war of economic liberation in motion. In a similar fashion, the modern jihad is a vehicle for the expansion of Islamist political and economic power. Once again, a single superpower, the United States, stands in the way of change and growth.

Economic forces, therefore, drove the First Crusade, though the rhetoric was religious; economic forces, cloaked in the language of jihad, today have inspired an Islamist crusade against the American Empire, an empire embodied in the economic hegemony that the West and its allies exercise over the Muslim world.

ECONOMIC DECAY, ECONOMIC CRUSADE

History can teach how to avoid making the same mistakes. The fall of the Roman Empire had disastrous consequences for the economies of Western Europe. The disintegration of the *Pax Romana* opened the gates to relentless looting by barbarian tribes; without the protection of Rome, entire regions were ransacked and their economies returned to pre-Roman conditions. Trade and commerce came to a halt and, almost overnight, what had once been a prosperous, buoyant economic system vanished. Money as a means of exchange disappeared, and economic transactions regressed to primitive barter agreements.

The feudal system that emerged from the disintegration of the Roman Empire rested upon the shoulders of peasants, who comprised 90 percent of Europe's population. Until the tenth century, closed subsistence economies built around agrarian settlements barely produced enough to feed the inhabitants, let alone enrich the nobility and the knights. From the eleventh century onward, improved agricultural tools (such as the introduction of the light plow) and an increase in farmland boosted production, but spectacular population growth more than absorbed the surplus and gave rise to serious food shortages.

Islamic economic domination during the Middle Ages contributed to the economic decay of Western Europe by hindering development and growth. During the ninth and tenth centuries, Islam enjoyed its commercial golden age, enriching merchants and states; in turn, trade spread Islamic culture all over the world. The Islamic economic domination of the Mediterranean turned Europe into a colonial and underdeveloped region, suffering from structural trade imbalances with the Muslim world. Europe's only exports were Frankish swords, Slavonic slaves, and English wool. In sharp contrast, imports from the East ranged from luxury items, such as silk and spices, to raw materials required for domestic industries, such as alum for fixing colors and dyes in textile. A constant drain of gold from West to East, to cover this trade imbalance depleted the European economy and reinforced its economic dependence upon Islamic regions.

Economic decay fostered conflict, which in turn destroyed productive resources. For centuries, Western Europe endured a constant state of war, attacked by Scandinavian, Eastern European, and Germanic tribes, as well as by Muslim armies. The barbarian invasions rendered the land useless. Irrigation systems and dams were destroyed, flooding large tracts of land. Any village unprotected by a lord and his castle fell prey to constant raids by soldiers and armed gangs. The church attempted to protect the poor by encouraging the construction of towns, but many lords opposed this strategy because they feared the new settlements would impinge upon their power. At the same time, extraordinary demographic growth placed mounting pressure upon villages, the resources of which became insufficient to sustain the growing population. "In this land you can scarcely feed the inhabitants," said Pope Urban II on the eve of the First Crusade. "That is why you use up its goods and excite endless wars among yourselves." Floods and pestilence swept through northwestern Europe in 1094, followed by drought and famine in 1095, making the situation even worse.

Then came Pope Urban II's call to arms to liberate the Holy Land at Clermont at the end of 1096. For the starving masses of Europe, the First Crusade offered a way of feeding themselves and an escape from a life of misery and suffering. For the knights and nobility, it offered an opportunity for economic expansion. Count Bohemund of Taranto is a case in point. Following the pope's call, Bohemund declared himself and his Norman troops "Franks," thus assuming the required ethnic identity to fight under the banner of Christianity, and sailed to the Holy Land. In reality, the Normans were neither Franks nor Christians, but descendants of the Vikings, the northern tribes that had ransacked and terrorized the Franks and other Western European tribes for centuries. The decision to embrace Christianity had been taken forty years earlier by Bohemund's forebears, brigands and mercenaries who had joined the Byzantine army to fight the Muslims. Taking advantage of the hostilities, the Normans had carved out a kingdom for themselves in southern Italy. From Sicily, a major crossroads for Muslim and Christian commerce, they saw in the First Crusade an opportunity for the eastward expansion of their domain. Christianity for the Normans was not a spiritual religion, but a vehicle for territorial conquest. Bohemund saw the Crusades as the driving force behind economic development, at the time synonymous with conquest, and the crusaders as the vanguard of this expansionary wave. Most of his fellow crusaders—the Franks' leaders, the knights, the militant clergy, even the peasants turned foot soldiers—shared this vision. The crusaders, aimed to free Europe of the economic hegemony of Islam, not to destroy Islamic civilization.

TWENTIETH-CENTURY REDUX

The modern jihad springs from an economic landscape similar to that of Western Europe at the time of the First Crusade, when Europe was a colony of Islam. Today the Muslim world feels equally subjugated to the West. Widespread demographic growth, coupled with progressive economic decay, has fuelled social unrest and conflict in the Muslim world; trade imbalances have drained resources from Muslim economies. Religion—this time Islam—provides the link for another uncommon alliance aimed at breaking an empire's economic hegemony.

In the twentieth century, the end of the *Pax Britannica* in the Middle East saw a carving up of the region and the disintegration of the preexisting order. Western powers and businesses continued to control oil and gas resources well after the decolonization process had occurred. This left deep marks in the Muslim world, sowing the seeds of a long-lasting economic and cultural Western hegemony. At the outset of decolonization, Western ideas continued to influence the politics and economics of Muslim countries. Some Arab leaders, like Egyptian President Gamal Abdel Nasser, admired the secularist elements of the West and applied them to force rapid modernization based upon the Western economic model. Others, like Saddam Hussein, turned their countries into bastions of Western secular civilization, bulwarks against Muslim countries such as Iran that dared reject these values.

While these leaders successfully applied Western economic principles, they did not introduce Western sociopolitical values such as representative democracy, a failure that facilitated the preservation of Western economic hegemony. The absence of democracy led to the creation of a new, immensely wealthy oligarchy: the Muslim elite. Educated and often raised in the

West, its members soon became the bridge between Western capitalism and Eastern resources and markets. The new Muslim oligarchy and Western capital formed partnerships and joint ventures with the aim of exploiting the resources and markets of the East. This alliance still controls the main trade flows between East and West: oil and gas flowing from the East, and Western manufactured goods flowing into the East.

The root of the structural imbalances that continue to characterize Muslim countries' economies lies in this economic alliance between the West and the Muslim oligarchic elites. Exports to the West are extremely limited and undiversified; oil and gas exports provide the bulk of foreign exchange earnings. Fluctuations in the world price and demand for these products regularly tilt the consolidated trade balance of Muslim countries. It is the ruling oligarchs' economic mismanagement and corruption, not market price fluctuations, that contribute most to sluggish economic growth and rising foreign debt.

A considerable percentage of oil-generated revenues never actually reaches Muslim economies. Some is diverted to the West; because oil-producing countries depend upon Western technology and markets, large shares of petroleum earnings have always gone to Western companies involved in oil exploration, exploitation, and trade in Muslim countries. Bin Laden has even calculated the amount of profits that Americans have accumulated from the sale of Arab oil. For every barrel sold over the last twenty-five years, he claims they pocketed $135. The total loss of income adds up to a staggering $4.05 billion per day, which he describes as the greatest theft in history. The magnitude of such a "swindle," he argues, entitles the 1.2 billion Muslims in the world to claim $30 billion each in compensation from America.

Another considerable part of foreign exchange earnings goes

to repay foreign debts or is legally invested abroad, predominantly in Western countries. Foreign investment has become yet another instrument in the hands of the Muslim elite to control the wealth of their countries and to prevent a more equitable distribution of it. The practice of legally investing abroad dates back to the mid-1970s when oil-producing countries used capital investment abroad to offset surpluses in their current accounts, surpluses which were generated by exports of oil and gas. This practice of recycling petrodollars—offsetting dollar outflows from Western countries' current accounts with dollar inflows into their capital accounts—began in 1973 after the first oil shock and was masterminded by Western banks, which were able to offer advantageous interest schemes to oil-producing countries for their capital investments.

Yet more money is taken out of Muslim countries illegally. Illegal capital flight involves funds secretly sent abroad—most commonly through trade mispricing (when invoices show a lower price)—with no record of transfer or existence in the country of origin. Because of its nature, illegal capital flight is difficult to quantify, but Raymond Baker of the Brookings Institution has estimated that today it is equivalent to 5 percent of the consolidated trade surplus of Muslim countries. The bulk of this money is laundered in the United States and Europe. This additional slice of foreign-exchange earnings taken out of Muslim economies feeds a structural drain of resources from Muslim countries to the West, similar to that experienced by Europe during the Middle Ages, and perpetuates economic dependence on the West.

In the 1990s, economic chaos in several Muslim regions, created by the collapse of the Soviet Union, provided new and fertile territory for Islamist recruitment. The example of the Fergana Valley in Central Asia illustrates this point. Government neglect and corruption in the 1990s turned the once fertile valley into a poverty-stricken area. Uzbek President Islam Karimov's blatant corruption and mismanagement destroyed the benefits of International Money Fund (IMF) loans. In April 2001, unable to convince Karimov to introduce economic reforms, the IMF withdrew from Uzbekistan altogether. Since then, capital flows have been meager. Karimov handles most deals himself and pockets large shares of the money. Unemployment in the Fergana Valley has reached 80 percent in recent years. With 60 percent of the population below the age of twenty-five, the valley has become an excellent recruitment ground for Islamist armed groups fighting the modern jihad. The leader of the Islamic Movement of Uzbekistan, Juma Namangani, killed during the 2001 war in Afghanistan, paid his men between $100 and $500 a month. A Northern Alliance fighter in Afghanistan, before the fall of the Taliban, could earn up to $250 a month and have access to food and cigarettes. Just as the Crusades presented the starving population of Europe with a chance for a better life, today the modern jihad offers people a way to feed their families and hope for the future.

THE RISE OF NEW CLASSES

Economic evolution, in the form of new commercial classes, also motivated both the Crusades and the rise of the modern jihad. Until the tenth and eleventh centuries, Arab and Jewish traders controlled commerce between Western Europe and Islam, and this trade had little, if any, positive impact upon the feudal social hierarchy of Europe. Then toward the end of the first millennium, the economic wasteland of Europe saw a new class of merchants, traders, and bankers emerge.

The rise of the Italian Maritime Republics of Amalfi, Pisa, Livorno, Genoa, and Venice gave new impetus to Italian merchants who became the vanguard of European commerce. They established the first commercial links with the East, importing silk and spices and exporting timber, iron, and cloth. This new class looked to the East as the natural arena for business expansion, but Muslim commercial supremacy stood in the way. All trade transactions with the East had to go through Arab or Byzantine traders, costly intermediaries who blocked direct access to Eastern and Far Eastern markets. Merchant fleets from the Italian Maritime Republics had to pay taxes and duties to the Arab fleets patrolling the Mediterranean Sea. Bankers, though willing to finance large trading businesses, were hindered by the limitations on European trade imposed by Arab domination.

By the time of the First Crusade, this new class of traders, merchants, and moneylenders, who had emerged from outside the ranks of the feudal system, began to demand centralized stability and the opening of new commercial routes to the rich markets of the East. To achieve this goal, they financed expeditions to reconquer the Holy Land. (Cities like Venice even manipulated the Fourth Crusade to gain control of new territories.) Thus, the Crusades cleared trade routes and contributed to the commercial revolution of Western Europe.

In the mid-1970s, the first oil shock and subsequent recycling of petrodollars created a new class of Muslim businessmen, traders, and bankers and boosted Islamic banking. Islamic banks sought to promote Islam by financing the development of infrastructure in the Muslim world and promoting a "new Islamic economic order." However, these institutions soon came up against the limits imposed by the economic hegemony of the West. The ruling Muslim oligarchy poured the bulk of its wealth into Western, rather than Islamic, banks as the latter were marginalized in international financial markets. Western interests and alliances with Muslim oligarchic elites also hindered the formation of a common Arab market along the lines of the European Economic Community and the introduction of a common Arab currency. But the fall of the Soviet system presented Islamic financiers and banks with vast new opportunities for growth. As Moscow severed its monetary lifelines, Islamic banks, predominantly from Arab countries and Iran, moved swiftly to fill the gap in Muslim areas in Central Asia, the Caucasus, and the Balkans, regions on the verge of economic chaos. They opened new markets for Muslim traders and businessmen and established strong commercial links. But Islamic bank loans went hand in hand with investments to build mosques and madrassas that prepared students to take part in the modern jihad. In this environment, Islamist armed groups blossomed.

Albania is a good example of this dynamic. In 1992, a delegation of the Turkish Islamic Development Bank (IDB) visited Tirana, laying the groundwork for strong economic cooperation between the two countries. Soon after this visit, Turkish trading companies began offering extremely advantageous contracts to Albanian importers and exporters. They took control of the market, pushing aside the International Fertilizer Development Center (IFDC) and the US advisory board formed to promote agricultural trade during Albania's transition to a market economy. The IFDC's mandate was to grant loans and supervise imports and exports. But Turkish and Arab traders backed by Islamic banks gradually pushed the IFDC out of the market entirely. Islamic financiers and banks also used the material support they provided to impose fundamentalist Muslim principles. A few months after the visit from the IDB, a delegation from Kuwait traveled to Albania and offered to implement an ambitious investment plan in exchange for permission to build several mosques. The Albanians readily accepted, and the Kuwaitis began building mosques and religious schools across the country. Various Muslim charitable organizations encouraged Albanian children to travel to Turkey, Syria, Jordan, Malaysia, Libya, Saudi Arabia, and Egypt by providing scholarships to study Islamic theology. According to the Helsinki Committee for Human Rights, Islamic missionaries in Albania took advantage of the spiritual and material crisis in the country to impose foreign models of extreme fanaticism, such as Wahhabism.

Muslim financial investments became an instrument for penetrating strategically important regions. In the mid-1990s, Iranian banks moved into Albania to establish an Islamist stronghold at the gates of Europe. Officially, the Iranian banks planned to invest in creating a support system for Albania, including banks, other financial institutions, charities, and humanitarian organizations, as well as the basic infrastructure necessary to sustain the economy. Secretly, Iran planned to establish a militant Islamist network in the country, within easy reach of Europe. Mohsen Nurbakan, the governor of the Central Bank of Iran (CBI), instructed domestic banks to invest in Albania regardless of poor profits or high risks. Iranian banking institutions soon became a primary source of hard currency in Albania. They provided links between local importers, exporters, and Islamic trading companies; they encouraged and facilitated trade with Iranian businessmen.

RELIGION AS IDENTITY

Why did the economic issues that underpinned the Christian Crusades find expression in a militant religious movement, and why is the same thing happening today in the Muslim world? Western Europe's despair in the eleventh century sprang from a crisis of political identity. With the disintegration of the Roman Empire, the church survived as the sole institution able to unite and protect Europe from the military expansion of Islam and of the Oriental hordes. Christendom was the only socioeconomic anchor available to the masses. Subordination to a set of Christian beliefs granted entry into society, and the identity of medieval Europe became largely synonymous with Christendom.

In the harsh economic conditions of eleventh-century Europe, the pope's call to arms invigorated a desperate population. The pope portrayed the enemy in its religious persona, focusing on the occupation of Jerusalem, the slaughter of Christians living or traveling there, and the profanation of the city where Christ died. He offered the hope not only of eternal salvation but also of immediate social transformation:

> Let those who for a long time, have been robbers, now become knights. Let those who have been fighting against their brothers and relatives now fight in a proper way against the barbarians. Let those who have been serving as mercenaries for small pay now obtain the eternal reward.

The people of Europe answered the pope's call to join the Crusades for a chance to feed themselves and gain riches looting the cities of the Islamic world. The nobility and knights, impoverished by centuries of war and economic decay, saw the Crusades as vehicles to mobilize the peasant tribes of Europe to conquer new lands and loot splendid cities. For the emerging merchant, trading, and banking classes, the Crusades represented a long-awaited opportunity to gain new markets. The papacy and the church, of course, saw an opportunity to gain more power and influence. Christianity gave these different groups a shared identity, and the Crusades brought them together to fight the stifling economic conditions in which they found themselves.

Today in the Muslim world, as the economic gap between the oligarchic powers of the elites and the masses widens, younger generations search for a sociopolitical identity. Religion, once again, offers unity and protection in the face of harsh and sometimes hopeless daily life. The success of the anti-Soviet jihad and its religious rigor have become symbols of Muslim strength. Islamist leaders today address packed mosques using rhetoric similar to that of Pope Urban II when he launched the First Crusade. For many Muslims in Central Asia, the Caucasus, Africa, and Southeast Asia, as well as those born in the industrial cities of Europe, Islam has become the principal referent of their identity. For these people, mosques around the world are socioeconomic refuges from deeply troubled waters.

Islamic fundamentalism has presented itself as a cohesive force, the sole power able to rid the Muslim world of Western economic hegemony. Emerging merchant, trading, and banking classes see in the modern jihad an opportunity to remove the impediments to business and economic growth imposed by Western domination. The masses see it as a chance to rid the Muslim world of parasitic elites and dictatorial regimes, opening up economic opportunities and restoring dignity to the Muslim world. The religious leadership sees it as a means of regaining political control over the Muslim world. The modern jihad is a brew of Islamist revolutionary ideology, a Muslim search for identity, and socioeconomic aspirations. Yet the rhetoric above all is religious, a rhetoric that once again dresses the enemy in clerical clothes and transforms an economically motivated conflict waged against a hegemonic power into a defensive jihad.

A search for identity during harsh times has intersected, then and now, with religious leaders' interest in reinforcing their authority. At the turn of the first and second millennia, Christianity and Islam, respectively, offered a cohesive identity to the masses stripped of their political and social beings by a hegemonic foreign empire. Pope Urban II helped channel economic and political desperation into a war between Christians and Muslims that transcended the political boundaries of Western Europe and relaunched the battered temporal power of the church. Through the modern jihad, Islamist leaders such as Osama bin Laden, the radical Saudi Islamist Abd al-Aziz bin Salih al-Jarbou, the Palestinian scholar Omar Abu Omar, and the former leader of the group Egyptian Islamic Jihad, Ayman al-Zawahiri, seek to ignite a global war of Muslims against Westerners, a war of religions. Their ultimate objective is to create one Arab nation united by Islam, a replica of the old Islamic caliphate, where temporal and religious powers come under a single Islamic authority. Bin Laden in particular, but others as well, have cleverly reshaped the terrifying aura of the Crusades and its association with the jihad, still deeply rooted in the Muslim collective imagination, into a propaganda and recruitment tool, transforming the confrontation with the hegemonic West into an Islamist crusade. By framing this modern jihad as a response to a new crusade, they have succeeded in extending the conflict to the greater enemy: the American Empire, the power that has prevented the removal of the corrupt Muslim rulers.

Behind their religious façades, the economic conditions and forces that set in motion the Crusades and the modern jihad are remarkably similar. The economic supremacy of Islamic and Western empires, at different times, has fostered economic decay and represented the major impediment to the growth of new emerging social classes that quickly identified a direct link between further economic opportunities and the end of the empire's hegemony. The Crusades and the modern jihad both represent wars of aggression against a dominant economic power. Both, in turn, triggered violent new conflicts in defense of the dominant status quo: Saladin's jihad and Bush's war on terror, respectively.

In response to the First Crusade, Saladin used the growing fear generated by the savage fighting of the crusaders to stir the dormant caliphate, and the concept of jihad to lay the necessary ideological ground for Muslims to rally around him. After the attacks of 9/11, the US administration ignited a new war in response, using the fear of future terrorist attacks to rally a nation prone to isolationism and unwillingness to support distant wars. While Saladin's jihad successfully defended the Islamic world for a short period, the Crusades marked the beginning of Europe's return to power. The prolonged conflict destroyed the tapestry of a society centered upon commerce and eroded the economy of the region. Likewise, the war on terror weakened the US economy to the extent that its economic leadership has come under scrutiny, a phenomenon that contributes to the magnitude of the current crisis.

CHAPTER 5

BLEEDING AMERICA BANKRUPT: BIN LADEN FULFILLS HIS DREAM

THE WAR AGAINST SYMBOLS: DESTROYING THE ICONS OF MODERN CAPITALISM

It takes but a moment to behead a hostage. A single swipe of the knife ends a human life. The job is fast and surprisingly clean, performed by the executioner in cold-blooded professionalism. Beheading by knife has been done before; during the anti-Soviet jihad in the 1980s, the mujahideen perfected this technique, executing hundreds of Soviet soldiers. In the 1990s, the method was exported from Afghanistan to Kashmir, Central Asia, Chechnya, and the Balkans—everywhere the mujahideen fought. Videos of Islamist warriors severing the heads of their enemies with knives circulated freely around the world; until 2003 they were on sale outside the Finsbury Park Mosque in London. Such videos, still available through underground channels, are powerful instruments of propaganda and recruitment for Islamist armed organizations.

The ritual slitting of a human throat bears a symbolic resemblance to the *zibah,* the Muslim procedure for slaughtering *halal* meat. In the zibah, the animal must be alive and healthy, as Islam forbids eating carrion. The slaughter is performed with a sharp knife, death is fast with minimal suffering, and a prayer of thanks to God accompanies the killing. Once the animal is dead, the blood is drained from the body. Because Islam considers blood haram, forbidden, the opposite of halal, bleeding is seen as an act of purification.

This simple, ancient ritual, performed daily in abattoirs across the world, is the allegoric key to the slaughtering of Western hostages. It also encapsulates one of the ultimate aims of the Islamist insurgency: to bleed the American economy until it is bankrupt.

JIHADIST SYMBOLISM

Images of hostages—chained, kept in cages, and decapitated like animals—have been posted to the Internet as powerful jihadist propaganda. The aim is "to give the West a taste of the degree of humiliation suffered by Muslims at the hands of Western powers," explained a Palestinian resident of Gaza. "The message being: this is how you have treated us for decades, like animals!"

The execution dehumanizes the victims and shocks the enemy. Men and women slaughtered as if they were halal meat—what could be more appalling to the highly civilized Western mind? But go back one thousand years and the roles are reversed. During the Crusades, similar acts of barbarism were committed against Muslims by the Frankish knights. The Frankish chronicler Radulph of Caen reports that in 1098, during the siege of Ma'arra, the crusaders "boiled pagan adults in cooking pots; they impaled children on spits and devoured them grilled." Tales of these atrocities spread across Islam and terrified a cultured and sophisticated civilization. Then, as much as today, fear was a potent strategic weapon.

Public executions proved similarly to be a powerful instrument of terror against the aristocracy during the French Revolution. With the guillotine as with the knife, a terrifying message is embodied in the lethal act and transmitted in its broadcast. Along the same lines, post-9/11 beheadings posted on the Internet created a widespread climate of panic that eroded the public's sense of security. The lack of a rational justification magnified the impact of those images. Just as the French nobility of 1789 was mystified as to why the population of Paris took pleasure in watching the guillotining of aristocrats in public squares, over the last years Westerners have not been able to comprehend the accumulated resentment that led some throughout the Muslim world to justify the execution of Western hostages.

Ultimately, ignorance is at the root of the failure to understand the enemy, and George W. Bush is a case in point. He never understood exactly what al-Qaeda really was: a bunch of religious fanatics, a proxy for a handful of Muslim governments, a network of terror financiers, the entire Muslim population engaged in a clash of civilizations? Nor did he understand the organization's goals: the recreation of the caliphate, the destruction of the House of Saud, the end of Western civilization? Unaware of the reasons for the hostility, one naturally assumes that no rational justification exists for such behaviour. When Marie Antoinette discovered that the people of Paris rioted because they had no bread, she suggested they should eat cake instead and stop shouting in the streets. Could she imagine that those rioters one day would behead her?

At the root of the economic violence of the credit crunch, once again one finds ignorance about the financial universe where our money is invested. Similarly, at the root of the nightmare scenario that politicians have depicted since 9/11, one finds ignorance about al-Qaeda and the jihadist movement. Politics and bad governance, not the economy, brought the current economic crisis upon us.

THE ECONOMIC CONSEQUENCES OF THE WAR ON TERROR

In 1998, al-Qaeda began attacking US interests in the Middle East. Since then a ritual similar to the beheading of hostages has taken place on a macroeconomic level.

Islamist terror has attacked the epicenter of Western capitalism, the American economy, in order to drain the wealth, essentially cutting off its lifeline. Symbolically, "bleeding America bankrupt" should purify the enemies of Islam by depriving the US and its allies of the power to back, both militarily and economically, the corrupt, oligarchic elites that rule most of the Muslim world. Over the last fifty years, these elites have impoverished their own populations while enriching themselves and contributing to the maintenance of Western economic hegemony in the Muslim world.

In the jihadist collective imagination, "bleeding America bankrupt" will weaken those elites and give Islamist insurgency a chance to overthrow them. This, in a nutshell, is the ultimate goal of Islamist terror, to replace corrupted Muslim regimes with a replica of the caliphate, a sociopolitical and socioeconomic system built on sharia law. Thus, the beheading of America's economy is the military strategy of a long-term war of economic liberation, which, like the Crusades, could last for generations. It was such an ideological stance that gave rise to the 9/11 attacks.

In the run up to 9/11, all this was empty rhetoric and wishful thinking; bin Laden and his organization realistically, were in no position to destroy the US economy. Paradoxically, though, after 9/11 these dreams did not seem so far-fetched after all because the US ingenuously fell into the ideological trap laid by bin Laden. After the tragedy of the twin towers, US rhetoric and propaganda magnified al-Qaeda's power exponentially. With utmost tenacity and determination, US propaganda led us to believe that a genuine, frightful enemy of enormous proportions, a ubiquitous foe, also nesting in Iraq, threatened America.

On 9/11, few knew that this was nothing more than political theater and that few Muslims had ever even heard of al-Qaeda. Moreover, Saddam Hussein's Iraq had no ties whatsoever to bin Laden. Saddam, as we have seen, feared Islamic fundamentalists as a force that contributed to his country's instability and thus threatened his own power. In addition to all this, the invasion of Afghanistan decimated al-Qaeda. Yet we believed what politicians told us.

Against this scenario, in August 2004, when the FBI discovered that al-Qaeda had gathered several reconnaissance videos of key economic targets inside the US, Washington once again stressed the power of the organization. Members, posing as tourists, had captured videos of economic icons, such as the New York Stock Exchange, the World Bank, and the IMF. FBI sources confirmed that the institutions were potential targets for future terror attacks. Yet documentation obtained by an influential Saudi newspaper suggests that prior to 9/11 Osama bin Laden had no intention to plan or launch a new attack against America. Instead he believed that 9/11 could be the last blow to destroy its economy and its power.

For al-Qaeda, targeting the twin towers, one of the icons of Western capitalism, went well beyond an act of symbolism. The attacks of 9/11 attempted to virtually decapitate the US economy. It was a sudden, shocking, professionally inflicted blow, broadcast live to the world.

THE PROLOGUE TO THE CREDIT CRUNCH

At a macroeconomic level, the impact was felt immediately as the sudden closure of markets hindered capital flows. Unable to liquidate their positions, US, foreign, and private investors watched considerable sums of money disappear from their portfolios; the Saudis alone lost $24 billion. When it became apparent that fifteen of the nineteen hijackers were from Saudi Arabia, Saudi investors rushed to repatriate the assets held in the United States. They feared personal, financial, and legal retaliation on top of the losses already sustained. As much as $200 billion, about a quarter of all Saudi investments in the US, left the country in the two months following the attack. Other Middle Eastern investors followed suit and drastically reduced their dollar-denominated investments for similar reasons. A year after 9/11, about $700 billion belonging to Muslim investors had left the US.

The most profound macroeconomic impact, however, came two months after 9/11, when the value of the dollar began to fall, slowing down American economic growth. While in the aftermath of the tragedy, markets reacted positively to Bush's war on terror—in fact, the dollar rallied—in the medium- and long-term, markets rejected Washington's policy. As the next chapter will show, the exodus of the dollar was also tied to the Patriot Act, a piece of legislation that imposed the monitoring of all transactions conducted in dollars.

By the end of 2001, global markets showed evident signs of nervousness vis-à-vis an overly aggressive US foreign policy. Investors' confidence in the Bush administration, therefore, began to falter. This happened at a time when the European Union, having recently adopted the euro as its common currency, provided a tangible alternative to the dollar. People began converting large portfolios from dollars into euros. Foreign investors' lack of confidence in Washington's war on terror, therefore, prompted an unexpected capital outflow from the US. Thus ended a decade of exceptional economic growth in the US (5.8 percent gross domestic product [GDP] per annum)—an economic boom fuelled largely by the continuous influx of foreign capital.

By early 2002, the US economy began to misfire or, to use bin Laden's preferred terminology, "started to bleed." Several prominent economists blamed the American president's war on terror. In 2003, Nobel Prize-winning economist Joseph Stiglitz painted a revealing new picture of America, a country impoverished by the folly of the war on terror. He showed that following 9/11 both consumption and growth plummeted— in 2003, US GDP was down to 3.5 percent. These figures today have a different meaning because we are facing a prolonged contraction of the economy. What they tell us, however, is that the current crisis started several years before the bubble burst.

The economic slowdown boosted unemployment. In 2002 and 2003, the number of jobs created fell short of the number of new entries into the labor market, leading to an overall loss in employment of 1 million jobs during Bush's first term. Such a figure had not been seen in America since the Great Depression. Naturally, these statistics seem very low compared to the catastrophic unemployment rate triggered by the credit crunch and the recession; during the last two months of Bush's second term, for example, another 1 million more Americans lost their jobs. Both of these figures, however, should make us reflect on the consequences of America's response to 9/11: the war on terror cost thousands of brave soldiers their lives and millions of Americans their jobs right from the start.

The slowdown in economic growth also caused a drastic reduction in benefits. To keep their jobs, workers accepted cuts in salaries. As a result, overall annual real household income in 2003 declined by $1,500. Americans' disposable incomes also shrunk, falling victim to high energy prices. According to Merrill Lynch, a 1¢ rise in the price of gasoline at the pump wipes out $1 billion from the pockets of US consumers, depriving the nation of extra liquidity that could be spent elsewhere. From 9/11 to the end of 2004, the price at the pump went from about one to two dollars per gallon. Apply Merrill Lynch's estimate to this increase and the effect is staggering: $100 billion vanished from American wallets.

Bush's first term represented the prelude to the credit crunch, yet at the time nobody foresaw what would come next. Neither Wall Street nor most of the American people showed concern about the economic consequences of the war on terror. Why? Perhaps it was because Alan Greenspan cleverly hid this fact behind the veil of a deflationary policy.

THE NEW ECONOMY OF TERROR

Greenspan's policy, while propping up a nation of borrowers, also became a boon to terror financiers, contrary to what the Patriot Act would lead us to believe. Indeed, from 9/11 onward, the new economy of terror continued to grow. Armed groups cunningly exploited Greenspan's deflationary policies to their advantage, and the bombardment of neocon propaganda to inflate al-Qaeda's powers turned out to be financially advantageous for terrorist organizations. Naturally, "Joe the Plumber" ignored these developments. To comprehend what happened, let's briefly revisit the basic structural elements of the international economic system based on violence.

The end of the cold war granted Western capitalism the possibility to spread across the entire planet. In the 1990s, deregulation removed economic barriers from international financial markets; capital, merchandise, and power began to circulate unimpeded. Likewise, armed groups profited from deregulation, and it became increasingly easy to do business with them.

Deregulation facilitated the merging of the terrorist economy with the illegal and criminal economies. This fusion gave birth to an international economic system with a GDP of $1,500 billion, exceeding the GDP of the UK. Its components are capital flight—about $500 billion moved clandestinely and illegally from country to country; the gross criminal product—another $500 billion generated by global crime; and the New Economy of Terror—$500 billion springing from terrorist organizations.

Of that $500 billion generated by terrorist organizations, one-third originates from legal activities, including donations, diaspora remittances, and salaries; the remaining two-thirds derive from criminal and illegal activities, drug trafficking being by far the most profitable. Al-Qaeda's finances were a fraction of the New Economy of Terror's annual turnover, especially when compared to the Irish Republican Army (IRA) or the Palestine Liberation Organization (PLO), both of which developed a flourishing economy in the territories they controlled, giving rise to shell states.

A shell state can be defined as an embryonic state, a proto-state. It possesses the economic infrastructure of a state, but not the political nucleus of a nation. The shell state lacks the right to self-determination—an example being the PLO and the Palestinians in Lebanon during the 1970s.

Shell states flourish in politically unstable environments, such as war zones. After 9/11, Afghanistan and Iraq became fertile grounds for the incubation and growth of shell states, at times even in areas no larger than a city block. After the fall of Saddam Hussein, Sadr City, a suburb of Baghdad, became a Shiite-controlled shell state. Others flourished in areas that had lost a central authority, as in Waziristan, the tribal area of Pakistan at the border of Afghanistan where bin Laden and the Taliban took refuge from 2001 onward. In Afghanistan, the district of Quetta is a shell state under Taliban control.

The dynamics that shape a shell state are always the same: A few armed groups conquer a territory by force and destroy its preexisting socioeconomic infrastructure, imposing their own. Meanwhile, the population remains trapped inside this territory, submitting to the violence or war economy only under duress. In Sadr City, Shiite militias patrol the streets conducting ethnic cleansing. They are responsible for attacks against Sunni families that have not yet abandoned their homes. They also run hospitals and schools. In short, they run the entire area. The goal is to compel the population to depend economically and socially on the economy of war thus forcing the people to become integral parts of the war economy itself. When the militia came to represent the sole authority able to ensure that Sadr City's economy kept functioning, the population in turn supported Muqtada al-Sadr's squads.

The 9/11 attacks gave rise to the proliferation of shell states throughout the Muslim world. The war on terror increasingly destabilized various key areas ranging from Iraq to Indonesia, the Horn of Africa to Pakistan, and the rest of the Middle East. At the same time, the response to 9/11 triggered escalating war expenditure across the Western world. The spread of power-hungry subversive groups, in fact, resulted in an upsurge of military interventions that boosted public spending and national debt.

While Bush's war on terror was sold as a virtuous attempt to export the principles of democracy to the Middle East, its impact was far from its sales pitch. Besides a death toll that includes a chilling number of civilian deaths throughout the Muslim world, this war sowed the seeds of political instability in several geographical areas while substantially inflating the trade deficit of Western countries.

Even more discouraging seem to be the pathetic results of the fight against the financing of terrorism, already discussed in Chapter 1. Financing proved to be the most dynamic sector of terrorism and the one that benefitted the most from globalization. Over the last few years, it has shown an uncanny ability to adapt to antiterrorist legislation, to mutate constantly, and to remain impervious to all measures devised to curb its growth.

Iraq and Afghanistan are prime examples of this dynamism. In June 2006, a report commissioned by the US government showed that the Iraqi insurgency had become financially self-sufficient. The term "Iraqi insurgency" is an umbrella that comprises the militia and private Shiite armies, Sunni armed groups, and jihadist members of al-Qaeda in Iraq.

At the onset of the war, these groups were funded with money from Saddam Hussein's vaults, donations from various jihad sympathizers and Iraqi exiles, and the governments of Iran and Saudi Arabia. Astonishing as it seems, according to the report, these monies are no longer needed. The insurgency has been able to produce about $200 million per annum, more than it needs to fund itself.

As of 2006, the Iraqi insurgency has been generating a profit, a surplus that many analysts consider large enough to finance terrorist activities abroad. Indeed, many believe that al-

Qaeda in Iraq partly bankrolled the Taliban military campaign launched in the spring of 2006, since al-Zawahiri previously had asked fellow al-Qaeda member Abu Musab al-Zarqawi to send money to Afghanistan.

How did the Iraqi insurgency manage to achieve economic self-sufficiency? The answer is simple: by exploiting a war economy entrenched in a globalized market and by taking advantage of the proliferation of shell states.

A US report identified three main sources of income: theft of imported oil, kidnappings, and the smuggling of weapons. Between 2004 and 2006, Iraq imported $4 to $5 billion worth of oil, of which about 30 percent was stolen and resold on the international and domestic black markets by armed groups and criminal gangs. The report also refers to a booming kidnapping industry. While the majority of those abducted are Iraqi, foreigners, especially journalists, are the most valuable.

Arms smuggling represents the third most profitable entry into Iraq's insurgency economy. Although Saddam Hussein did not possess any weapons of mass destruction, he owned the second largest arsenal of small arms in the world after the US. When his regime fell, terror and criminal groups ransacked this arsenal. Using their links with organized crime, these groups sold Iraqi armaments widely, with arms reaching Somalia, Sudan, and Lebanon by 2006.

This same model of self-funding can be found in Afghanistan. Terrorism post-9/11 requires fewer and fewer external financiers while counterterrorism balloons. The two seem to grow in inverse proportion. After 9/11, Pakistan's Inter-Services Intelligence (ISI), along with Islamic fundamentalist tribal leaders, bankrolled al-Qaeda and the Taliban leadership that had gone into hiding in Waziristan. Paradoxically, part of the US foreign aid negotiated by Pakistan in exchange for its support found its way into the Taliban's and al-Qaeda's pockets via the tribal leaders. These funds, however, soon became superfluous.

From 2002 until 2006, the reconstituted Taliban army and al-Qaeda got their finances in shape. They established their headquarters at Quetta, a medium frontier city that soon became a shell state. Quetta is an important counterfeit market for the region; all types of knockoffs can be found in the city. Quetta is also an important hub for Central Asia's booming smuggling business and has become increasingly known for kidnappings. In 2006, the Taliban released an Italian journalist in exchange for six Taliban prisoners and, most likely, a sizeable ransom.

Unlike the Iraqis, the Taliban also have a renewable natural resource at their disposal: drugs. Booming opium production is funding their offensive. In 2006, the opium harvest was 35 percent greater than the previous year. By 2008, Afghanistan was producing 92 percent of the opium sold on the global market. Before 9/11, its market share amounted to less than 70 percent.

Bush's apocalyptic war rhetoric had yet another pernicious and disquieting effect: the declining cost of terrorist activities in the West. The 9/11 attacks cost al-Qaeda $500,000, while the Madrid massacre cost only $20,000, and the London suicide bombings less than $15,000. Osama bin Laden no longer operates costly training camps but relies upon the proliferation of jihadist websites to indoctrinate and train a new generation of jihadists at rock-bottom prices.

The real danger lies in the transformation of al-Qaeda from a small armed faction into a global anti-imperialist ideology: "al-Qaedism." This disturbing turn of events springs precisely from the war in Iraq.

In the jihadists' collective imagination, 9/11 represents an iconic event and, simultaneously, the blueprint for future attacks. All that has changed since that tragic event is the money available and the professionalism of those who wish to emulate it. The attacks of Istanbul, Madrid, and London are smaller-scale replicas of 9/11. Yet their respective impacts on public opinion were vast and resounded across the globe. After each attack, the Western propaganda machine switched into ever-higher gear and magnified the powers of those who carried out the attacks, blowing them completely out of proportion. As we shall see, the specter of fear greatly enhanced the impact of political violence in our collective imagination.

Political propaganda and the press kept tensions running high even during periods of relative calm. In 2004 and 2005, FBI sources insisted that the highly symbolic institutions of Western capitalism were still targets of al-Qaeda: a gross assessment error. As mentioned before, after the attack in Afghanistan, al-Qaeda was no longer in any position to repeat an act of aggression of this magnitude. Nonetheless, alarms periodically went off in Washington and New York, entire buildings were evacuated, and the cities remained paralyzed for several days.

If we apply a cost-benefit analysis to the war on terror, its disastrous outcome would become evident. Far from having brought peace to the world, the war on terror hatched an asymmetric conflict. While $200 million has been more than enough to sustain the Iraqi insurgents, Washington's war costs have run in the trillions. The monthly Pentagon budget for Iraq amounts to $8 billion, $12 billion if we add Afghanistan.

In response to the rising costs of the war, Washington cut interest rates and sold off treasury bonds internationally. The credit crunch and the economic quagmire inherited by Barack

Obama prove the folly of this strategy. The financing of the war now competes directly with the plans to rescue the American economy. What is more important: to export democracy "made in America" or to save America itself? This is the agonizing question, similar to the one confronting Hamlet, that Obama faces.

Bush's legacy is an open-ended, asymmetrical war to manage a potentially unresolvable conflict that sucks money and lives from the state and the taxpayer without contributing anything to peace and to the economy. In a recession as serious as the present one, the maintenance of this war against enemies of our own creation diverts resources desperately needed to sustain America's and the world's economies.

Obama's new American rhetoric is insufficient to solve these problems. What is badly needed is a radical plan of action, both for foreign policy and for the economy, the two main components of the recession. Why has deregulation not been tamed yet? Wall Street is as free and unregulated as it was before the credit crunch. Our money is equally at risk. The US Congress may not be ready for the badly needed reforms, and this could be a problem for America and the world.

One must remember, the president represents only the tip of the iceberg, one that breaks off at least every two terms. As popular as Obama may be, his leadership will last only four to eight years. Congress holds the reins of the nation and designs the greater picture of domestic and foreign politics; Congress represents the people, a nation that still does not have a clear picture of what went wrong. To complete this complex puzzle, let us analyze the disturbing ties between the war on terror and other aspects of the economy: money laundering and the credit crunch.

CHAPTER 6

THE USA PATRIOT ACT:
A SELF-INFLICTED WOUND

MONEY LAUNDERING US DOLLARS

Until 9/11, the currency of choice of the terror, illegal, and criminal economies was the greenback, the preferred banknote being the Ben Franklin, the hundred-dollar bill. Every year, a large percentage of the total turnover of the black economy—valued at about $1.5 trillion, roughly 5 percent of the global economy—was laundered inside the US through a series of well-established recycling mechanisms.

It is no surprise that the majority of these funds found their way into the US via tax havens scattered in Central America and the Caribbean. According to the Brookings Institution, until 2001 more than 80 percent of the dirty money produced across the globe transited through these offshore facilities. No monitoring of cash flows took place. The sensational tales of mafioso traveling to the Cayman Islands or Bermuda in private jets or on luxury yachts with suitcases stuffed with cash are all true.

Everybody knew that this business did not exist only in the imagination of the creator of *Miami Vice*, yet no one spoke about it openly. Government silence, however, is explained easily enough: money laundering injected the American economy with cash while simultaneously boosting the domestic money supply, a mechanism essential to running a ballooning debt.

With the dollar as the world's reserve currency, the US can borrow against the amount of its currency in *global* circulation. While all other nations are restricted to the amount in circulation in their domestic economy, for the US the planet is the limit. No other nation has this privilege, referred to as seignorage, the exclusive prerogative of the country issuing the reserve currency. Therefore, the recycling of illicit and dirty money in dollars inside the US offered Washington access to even greater indebtedness; indeed, these flows actually reinforced American economic prospects.

The peculiar link between the American economy and the black market has been cemented over several decades. Statistics from the Federal Reserve show that from the mid-1960s onward, an ever-increasing number of dollars left the country every year without ever coming back. In 2000, one-third of newly printed money, amounting to about $500 billion, was smuggled out to feed the demand for dollars in the illegal, terror, and criminal economies. For years, the extent of the interdependence between criminal activity–related monetary flows and the American economy has reached far beyond money laundering alone, becoming integral to the credit capacity of the country itself. Yet nobody has attempted to sever such disturbing ties.

This scenario changed quite suddenly in October 2001, when Congress approved the Patriot Act. From this juncture, the US slipped into an irreversible downward spiral of unmanageable debt. Money supply slowed down and with it the possibility to borrow. The only response that Alan Greenspan and the Fed could devise was a policy of aggressively low interest rates to raise yield on government bonds, a measure which in turn made them more competitive. It was only a quick fix to deal with a crisis that threatened to seep into US politics.

This last-ditch strategy for survival soothed the short-term symptoms of an ailing economy but had devastating long-term effects that worsened as the cuts continued. It created the ideal conditions for the aggressive sale of subprime mortgages and damaged the already overheated American and Western economies. Today we are witnessing its tragic final consequences.

EUROPE: MONEY LAUNDROMAT TO THE WORLD

The Patriot Act (the common phrase for the USA PATRIOT Act of 2001, which stands for Uniting and Strengthening America by Providing Appropriate Tools Required to Intercept and Obstruct Terrorism) brought unexpected changes to the sick partnership between the US economy and the money-laundering business. The drastic post 9/11 anti–money-laundering regulations added severe controls and conditions to American finance. As a result, the US ceased to be the epicenter of money laundering. But as the flow of dirty and illegal money declined, the global turnover of US dollars decreased. Paradoxically, well before this legislation struck a blow at the presumed terrorists, it began to wreak havoc at home.

In essence, the financial segment of the Patriot Act is a legislation intended to curb money laundering. It prohibits US banks and US-registered foreign banks from conducting business with tax havens and offshore banks. Simultaneously, it bestows upon US authorities the power to oversee all dollar transactions across the globe and to penalize institutions that do not report suspect dollar transactions anywhere in the world. Since October 2001, many banks have been penalized, including European institutions like UBS and Lloyds TSB Bank.

THE EXODUS FROM THE GREENBACK

The Patriot Act wreaked almost immediate devastation on the US economy. As early as November 2001, a downward trend could be observed in both legal and illegal dollar transactions. The international banking community did not like the compulsory monitoring of funds. Neither did it appreciate the fact that the US was able to pursue them legally. In addition, banks had to absorb costs associated with the implementation of the new regulations, such as ongoing training for employees to stay abreast of the continual changes and updates. Eventually, larger international banks began to encourage their clients to avoid, or to divest themselves of, dollars and dollar investments.

Prior to 9/11, Muslim investors who held about $1,000 trillion in the US featured among the first to abandon the greenback. Soon others followed suit. This exodus further weakened US currency, and the demand for US dollars dropped steadily while other currencies prospered. By the end of November 2001, the dollar began to depreciate while the money launderers' move overseas to Europe further exacerbated the imbalance between dollar demand and supply, sapping the American economy.

As the global demand for dollars declined, the supply of new money in the US decreased. As a consequence, the ceiling of American borrowing capabilities came down. With monetary growth slowing, the relationship between the GNP and public debt shifted, as the former dwindled and the latter grew. Treasury bonds became less competitive and thus more difficult to sell on the international market. To bear the weight of a rising public debt, the Federal Reserve performed a series of drastic interest rate cuts to shore up bond values. Rates fell from 6 percent on the eve of 9/11 to 1.2 percent at the beginning of the summer of 2003. During this interval, the seeds of the credit crunch were sown. Thus the Patriot Act set in motion an unexpected chain reaction on a global economic scale that sealed America's response to 9/11 to the destiny of the world economy.

UNEXPECTED GROWTH OF THE BLACK MARKET

Ironically, the one thing that the Patriot Act did not achieve was the curbing of terrorism financing. This should come as no surprise, though, as the legislation was evidently not devised as an antiterror measure. If this statement appears preposterous, think again. The proof lies in the fact that, since its implementation, only a trifling $200 million has been blocked—a pittance in a $500 billion economy. What *is* surprising is that even the effects observed on the money-laundering front seem very modest. The reason is simple: the Patriot Act is applied only in the US and refers only to the dollar. International crime syndicates responded promptly to the legislation and moved their money-laundering enterprises to Europe. As a consequence, the Patriot Act inflicted damage on the European economy as well.

This smooth transition to the euro was made possible by the absence of any similar European legislation. No homogenous and overarching structure with which to prevent money laundering or to regulate tax havens still existed within the European Union. Due to permissive fiscal policies and an abundance of offshore facilities, Great Britain soon turned into a tax haven. For example, in 2004, Saudi funds from Dubai, which were destined for a radical mosque located in Milano's Via Quaranta, arrived in Europe via offshore banks in the Channel Islands.

THE RISE TO POWER OF THE ITALIAN 'NDRANGHETA

The Patriot Act also forced Colombian drug cartels to find new routes to conduct their business. The drug lords feared the international monitoring of dollar transactions. Their fundamental problem was not the recycling of their illicit profits but rather the physical transfer of cash between countries and the subsequent investment of these monies away from the control of US monetary authorities. After 9/11, the cartel tightened its business alliance with 'Ndrangheta (an Italian organized crime syndicate centered in Calabria) thanks to a Sicilian immigrant, Salvatore Mancuso, who had become the leader of the Colombian paramilitary organization United Self-Defense Forces of Colombia (AUC). With Mancuso as the link between these two organizations, 'Ndrangheta offered full service to the drug lords: drug smuggling, money laundering, and legitimate investments in euros.

In 2002, the euro was still the new kid on the currency block, but the amazing opportunities it offered were immediately evident to organizations involved in the recycling of dirty money, including 'Ndrangheta. The euro greatly facilitated the transport and exchange of cash within the EU, preventing law enforcement officials from being able to identify the origins of illegal revenue. In fact, statistics released by the Italian *Guardia di Finanza* demonstrate that money laundering increased 70 percent in Italy between 2001 and 2004.

In the past, 'Ndrangheta had used tourist foreign exchange agencies for laundering purposes, but these operations cost 50

ITL per dollar, not to mention the time required for the conversion. The advent of the euro facilitated the transfer of large quantities of cash between European countries at a vastly reduced cost. Recent Europol statistics confirm that since 2001 there has been an upsurge in banknotes circulating within the EU territory. The absence of any EU regulation requiring the declaration of cash as it flows in and out of its territory has inadvertently encouraged wholesale shipments of money. During the 2005 operation code-named "Chub," British customs officers in Dover intercepted a freezer truck en route from Great Britain to Central Europe. Inside was a cache of £3.5 million sterling in cash derived from drug trafficking, destined for investment in Spanish, Italian, and Greek real estate.

Europol has reported that a network of European attorneys and accountants, in collaboration with real estate agents, is at the heart of an operation that uses European real estate markets to launder immense quantities of dirty money. Given the absence of any system for the exchange of real estate transactions across European borders, tracing the origin of the operation's assets has proved to be quite difficult.

THE WAR ON TERROR: AN ECONOMIC FOLLY

It is quite clear that the Bush administration launched the war on terror without properly considering the potential economic consequences. Paradoxically, the Bush administration's response to 9/11 has helped fulfill—at least in part—bin Laden's absurd dream of bleeding the American economy to death. More to the point, the Patriot Act did not curb the financing of terrorism, but it did end up debilitating the American economy and turning Europe into the world's money laundromat.

Meanwhile, the cost of maintaining military efforts on two

fronts has negatively impacted US public debt. Even Republicans admit that the weapons employed to deliver the *coup de grâce* to the enemy have actually weakened the American economy. Pat Buchanan is one of these critical voices. In his book entitled *Right Went Wrong*, he describes Bush's foreign policy as "democratic imperialism" and predicts that such policies would not only drive the country into bankruptcy but would also isolate the US from the rest of the world.

Buchanan draws an interesting parallel between the cost of the war on terror and the deficit accumulated during the Vietnam War by the Johnson administration. In 1968, at the height of the war, the military machine cost the public treasury the equivalent of about 9.3 percent of the GDP. In comparison, the cold war cost the taxpayer, on average, 6 percent of the GDP. By the summer of 2004, Bush's military expenses were already approaching 5 percent of the GDP. Obama inherited a public debt amounting to 70 percent of the nation's GDP.

Unfortunately, Buchanan's prognoses turned out to be correct. In the summer of 2007, before the banks were bailed out, US public debt represented 40 percent of the GDP, due largely to military expenditure and the cost of domestic security. In fact, the Pentagon's annual budget swelled from $420 billion in September 2004 to $700 billion in September 2008. US defense spending is double the combined total of the fifteen nations with the highest military expenditure in the world, including the UK.

The economic consequences of the Vietnam War are well known yet worth revisiting. The years of drawn-out conflict resulted in a substantial increase of public debt, inflation, and, subsequently, recession. Today, the US and world economies seem to be caught in a similar dynamic: facing increasing public debt and oil and raw material price hikes, the nation has allowed the recession to creep into every home. Buchanan argues even more emphatically that Bush's war on terror will lead the country into bankruptcy because the military effort is unsustainable. The author suggests that this miscalculation is so huge that in the end it could work to the advantage of the jihadist insurrection and to the disadvantage of the world's economy. To paraphrase Buchanan: a massive drop in tax revenues accompanied by a very costly war is invariably a prelude to disaster.

The impact of the Vietnam War was felt first and foremost in the international market. The conflict ended up exhausting the country's gold reserves, forcing Nixon to declare an end to the convertibility of the dollar. This marked the end of the gold-exchange standard, an exchange system in which only the dollar had parity in gold, thus serving as benchmark and anchor, in monetary terms, for all the other currencies. This triggered a profound monetary crisis as the world was forced to adapt to a system of constantly fluctuating rates of exchange.

Today, as it happened then, the most disastrous repercussions of Washington's errors befall the entire planet. The first telltale signs of the recession, which threaten to foment the rise of protectionist pressures all over the world, were already visible in the mid-2000s in the energy and food crises.

CHAPTER 7

OIL AS A RETALIATORY WEAPON

1973 DÉJÀ VU

"We live day by day, processing information and news by the hour. In this political climate it seems impossible to make any forecast. Who can guarantee that stability will prevail from one day to the next? Even so, one faces the Saudi variable: the danger of new attacks against the world's largest oil producing country," lamented the manager of one of Canada's largest energy investment funds, shortly after the first democratic election in Iraq. From 9/11 to 2005, when strong speculation sustained oil prices' exceptional climb, the barometer of energy costs did not respond to the fundamentals of economics but was sensitive to the ups and down of the war on terror.

In the aftermath of the attack, crude oil prices went through the roof. This happened after a decade of relative stability. What were the causes? The attacks of 9/11 certainly did not change the fundamentals of economics. Political and emotional factors caused the price hike. The market reacted badly to Washington's exploitation of the threat of terrorism, a propaganda campaign stoking the politics of fear to justify its preemptive strike against Iraq. Against this backdrop, market operators feared a scenario similar to the infamous thirteen days in 1973, one of those unique events that changed the course of economic history.

On October 6, 1973, Egypt and Syria simultaneously attacked the territories that Israel had seized in 1967, marking the beginning of the war of Yom Kippur. Ten days later in Washington, Henry Kissinger, secretary of state under President Richard Nixon, dismissed the idea that the Arabs would use oil as a weapon to retaliate against the US for supporting Israel. The next day he was proven wrong. Nine Arab ministers from the Organization of the Petroleum Exporting Countries (OPEC) met in Kuwait and agreed to slash oil supply. They stipulated an immediate 5 percent monthly reduction of oil exports to "unfriendly" nations, those that sided with Israel, and the progressive, total reduction of oil exports to the US. The embargo started on October 19, and within a few days the price of oil quadrupled.

Thirty years later, in the midst of the war on terror, a similar fear tormented the financial market: could oil, once again, be used as a retaliatory weapon? As in the OPEC crisis, oil prices became decoupled from supply and demand, the fundamentals of economics. Rather, prices were at the mercy of political variables. One fundamental difference, however, distinguished the energy crisis of the new millennium from the oil embargo. In 1973, OPEC, a legitimate organization, controlled oil supply. In the early 2000s, a largely unknown and elusive enemy—Islamic terrorism—influenced oil prices. Total uncertainty gripped the markets. "It is as if playing a three-dimensional chess game while seeing only in 2-D. One is never quite able to anticipate the adversary's next move," said Filippo Cortesi, former director of the financial derivatives section of CDC IXIS, a French bank in London.

Today, as in 1973, markets must respond to unpredictable factors. Yet this time around, uncertainty has become the rule. Far from being a quick war, the war in Iraq mutated into a gruesome civil war and fomented terrorist activities across the Muslim world, including in Saudi Arabia.

THE DANGER OF FEAR

Even today, the role that Islamic fundamentalists actually played in Iraq and the full extent of al-Qaeda's power in Saudi Arabia are still unclear. In 2004, Prince Turki, then Saudi ambassador to the UK, reassured the world that inside his country al-Qaeda was practically defeated. Yet organizations monitoring Saudi stability contradicted this statement. In 2004, Merchant International Group, a political risk consultancy, forecasted an escalation of terrorist attacks in Saudi Arabia and stated that Saudi security forces failed to manage, let alone defeat, the threat of al-Qaeda. Though none of these predictions came true, the market took them onboard and the price of oil increased each time similarly gloomy forecasts flashed on the monitors of the dealing rooms.

Political propaganda, streaming directly from al-Qaeda's terror network, contributed to the skittishness of the market. Worrisome communiqués posted on the Internet, urging followers to harm the Western economy, boosted uncertainty about the future of oil. Osama bin Laden proved to be quite a crafty propagandist. Newspapers and politicians incessantly interpreted messages from him and his followers, and the threat of terrorism seemed more imminent every day.

Bin Laden clearly understood oil's potential as a retaliatory weapon against the global economy, but he also realized that an embargo would not be used again. Unlike in 1973, now

Arab leaders need Washington's economic and military support to fulfill their ambitions. However, fear alone could go a long way toward fulfilling bin Laden's goals. The fear of the embargo was as potent as the embargo itself. Inside international markets fear was endemic. To maintain it at a high level, and let people believe that an interruption of supply from Saudi Arabia could come at any moment, in 2003 bin Laden revoked a fatwa that forbade his followers to attack targets in Saudi Arabia. The market reacted immediately, and oil prices went through the roof.

Osama bin Laden has been well aware that since 1979 the alliance between OPEC and the West has hinged on Saudi Arabia's role within the oil cartel. The Saudis practically run the world's oil bank. In times of crisis they increase oil supply, as happened in the aftermath of the Iranian Revolution and the Gulf War. Their role in ensuring the delicate stability of oil prices has become crucial, and for that reason the terrorist threat against Saudi Arabia unnerved the West. "An attack against Ras Tanura, from where about 80 percent of Saudi exports sail, would make the market go haywire," remarked George Magnus, economic advisor of USB London, in 2004. In the collective imagination of oil traders, such hypothetical threats—reinforced almost daily by al-Qaeda's propaganda—became real and imminent.

Forecasters suggested that a regime change or even a spectacular al-Qaeda attack inside Saudi Arabia would push oil prices past the barrier of one hundred dollars per barrel, equivalent to the 1979 peak reached in the aftermath of the Iranian Revolution. But these forecasters were mistaken. Fear of terrorism and its by-product—uncertainty—drove prices well beyond this barrier. Above all, insecurity paved the way for speculators, who, along with international banks, invaded the raw materials market in 2005. From then on, widespread speculation pushed the price of crude oil up to $150 per barrel. The anomalies of an unregulated and out-of-control economy, unresponsive to the economic fundamentals of supply and demand, were the root causes of the oil price hike.

Soon the hike spread like a contagion to other sectors. Before the credit crunch and after 9/11, the commodity market began to absorb a large part of the world's liquidity. Banks, stockbrokers, hedge funds, and private investors flocked to this market *en masse*, seeking their piece of the pie. This phenomenon helped inflate the financial bubble, and the post-9/11 fear of terrorism created the favorable conditions for this to happen.

FUTURES OF FEAR

During the first years of the new millennium, nobody saw what was happening. Even the oil futures market, which did not exist in 1973, could not offer any useful indication. "Futures markets," explained Cortesi, "act as a barometer of the level of prices to come. They respond to variation of supply and demand. If a product becomes scarce, because either global demand increases or supply diminishes, for example, the futures go up in price." Yet nobody could understand why prices kept rising while supply and demand remained relatively stable. From 9/11 on, political factors governed the oil market. In May 2004, the attacks on Yanbu and Khobar in Saudi Arabia did not affect Saudi oil production and export but triggered a race to buy futures contracts. Speculators and companies that heavily depended on oil purchases, such as airlines, became front-runners in the race. This was a clear sign that speculators had gotten a whiff of new market opportunities.

In the spring of 2004, Merrill Lynch published a document

stating that the speculative demand—long-term oil contracts held by investment funds—had reached historic high levels of 124 million barrels. The market had not seen such numbers since the First Gulf War. Hedge funds and investment banks alike had moved huge sums into the oil futures market, pushing up oil prices and, in turn, increasing the cost of virtually all consumer goods. Increased prices were the cost of fear, not scarcity.

Paradoxically, in June 2004, when attacks on two oil pipelines that supplied the oil terminals in Basra paralyzed Iraqi exports, the market remained quiet. Overnight, up to 1.6 million barrels per day disappeared from the world market, not to reappear for weeks, and yet the price of crude oil futures barely twitched: it rose a meager eleven cents, a tiny fraction of the five-dollar increase reported after the attack on Khobar, Saudi Arabia, a few months earlier.

From 9/11 until the end of 2004, fear of terrorism guided the hike in the price of crude oil—though did not, as many believed, increase demand from China and India. That explains why increases in OPEC's oil production proved to be mere palliatives. The problem was psychological, not structural. Uncertainty continued to prevail.

"We do not know what lurks around the corner," remarked Susan Johns, a Canadian energy fund manager, in the fall of 2004, before the price per barrel shot up.

WHO BENEFITS FROM A WEAK DOLLAR?

Another element that contributed to the hike in oil prices was the weakening of the dollar. Oil-producing countries increased prices to compensate for losses incurred from the steadily depreciating American currency.

Although the dollar's slump contributed to global economic imbalance, the Bush administration found it convenient and did not attempt to stop its decline. In 2007, the US trade deficit fell from 7 percent to 5.5 percent of the GNP, and the budget deficit also shrank. A weaker currency boosted imports, reducing the debt by forcing Washington to become more frugal. Thus the United States regained its position as the world's second largest exporter, rivaled only by China, a ranking it had lost during the first and most of the second term of the Bush administration.

Underlying the politics of the weak dollar, one finds a strategic compromise between China and the US, two countries bound by a complex business relationship: China being the world's biggest exporter and largest underwriter of US debt, and the US being the largest importer of Chinese goods. Chinese money, through this convoluted channel, financed Bush's war on terror.

In 2003, the US started to pressure Beijing to revalue the yuan—which it said was artificially low—to reduce the competitiveness of Chinese imports. China, however, turned a deaf ear to these requests and instead purchased dollars on the market to counter the pressure to revalue that derived from the trade surplus. By the end of 2007, the Chinese central bank had accumulated about $1.5 trillion in its reserves, exceeding even the $1 trillion held by Japan. This stockpile proved quite valuable a year later when the credit crunch hit.

Washington's answer was to allow the dollar to weaken. The rationale: if the Chinese refuse to revalue, then we devalue. The weak dollar, however, damaged Europe. From the end of 2001 to 2007, the exchange rate climbed from $0.86 to $1.45 per euro. European exports to the US suffered greatly.

Indirectly, though, Europe also benefitted from the weakening dollar because it purchased oil and natural gas with dollars. In 2007, the devaluation of the greenback actually compensated for the hike in oil prices, so that for those who purchased oil in euros, the price remained pretty much the same.

Toward the end of 2007, Venezuelan President Hugo Chávez made note of this anomaly during an OPEC meeting and tried to persuade other OPEC members to set prices in euros rather than dollars. Iran's President Mahmoud Ahmadinejad, who had been quoting crude oil prices in euros for years, supported Chávez's suggestion, which was another episode of Chávez's anti-US propaganda. Switching from the dollar to the euro is easier said than done. Even though Iran quotes oil prices in euros, payments still take place in dollars because all commodity transactions take place in dollars, so why make them more expensive through an exchange rate?

Despite Chávez's and Ahmadinejad's propaganda, 2007 proved too early to talk about ending the role of the dollar as the reference currency of the world economy. Technical difficulties would have to be overcome: if the euro took over the role of the dollar, the European Central Bank would not be able to meet the sudden increase in the demand for euros. There are simply not enough euros in circulation in the world to satisfy such a demand, and to print more banknotes would cause inflation to rise across the EU. The war on terror clearly eroded the dollar's supremacy but its replacement is, by sheer necessity, slow in coming.

WHY IS THE WORLD HUNGRY?

In the spring of 2008, the United Nations declared that the surge in food prices could potentially cause the starvation of more than 1 billion people. Like during the Irish Potato

Famine, the culprits of the 2008 food crisis were neither famine nor natural disasters but rather food prices. In Haiti and Cairo alike, people took to the streets demanding food, yet local supermarket shelves were filled with goods too expensive to buy. In India, a rice-exporting country, 1 million Indian citizens risked starvation.

Like the energy crisis, the food crisis rested not on structural factors, such as increased demand from Asia, developing countries' dependency on imported food, grain shortages in Australia, or the increase of biomass-energy production. Instead, hordes of speculators invading future markets prompted the inflation. Of course, the price of oil did contribute, since 60 percent of agricultural costs depend on the price of energy. Speculators, therefore, simultaneously gambled on the devaluation of the dollar and the increase of oil prices.

Futures markets, paradoxically, were originally created to protect both producers and consumers with buffers against price fluctuations and changes in interest and exchange rates. Futures contracts became widespread in the food and agriculture sectors, as they are an insurance of sorts. In order to avoid losses incurred by price fluctuations, farmers acquire seeds or sell grains in three- or six-month intervals at prices negotiated at a specific time, more often than not at harvest. Multinational corporations like Kraft and Nabisco acquire agricultural futures for the same reasons. When the transaction occurs, the decision to exercise the futures contract is made, depending upon the direction in which the prices are going.

Speculators neither sell nor buy anything; profits are made simply via fluctuations of the prices of these contracts. These are transformed into stocks and bonds via derivatives applied to stock market indices that take over their rating. These products are then traded on the secondary market and renewed before they reach maturity. This process is called a rollover, a renewal of these futures, and it forms the basis of speculative profit making.

In a market with soaring prices, a quarterly grain-purchasing agreement made in January 2007 not only increased in value each time the price of grain went up but could also be renewed ad infinitum. The race to purchase these futures led to price increases, inflating the speculative demand without ever creating any actual scarcity. This explains the anomaly of a food shortage in a world in which there is plenty of food to feed everyone.

Until 2000, restrictions were in place for the speculative use of futures markets in order to avoid manipulations and imbalances like those witnessed in the spring of 2008. But deregulation managed to abolish those restrictions. From that point onward, speculators invaded the agricultural futures market. Congress was presented the following data by Michael Masters, a US hedge fund manager: speculation increased from $13 billion in 2003 to $260 billion in 2008. In April 2008, this amounted to 35 percent of all corn futures, 42 percent of soy seeds, and 64 percent of grains. In 2001, all these percentages were below 10 percent.

Money makes the world go 'round—at all costs—even if this means letting much of its population go hungry. The culprits are among a new class of financiers who have held the reins of global finance ever since the fall of the Berlin Wall. The war on terror created a culture of uncertainty that these financiers found ripe to exploit. They are the "Masters of the Universe" as described in Tom Wolfe's *Bonfire of Vanities*, the bankers that led global finance into the abyss of recession, and after September 11, 2001, London turned into their new headquarters.

CHAPTER 8

SCENES FROM THE GLOBAL HOUSE OF CARDS

LONDON: METROPOLITAN ICON OF THE WEST

Until recently, each morning between 8:30 and 9:30 a.m. London's Chelsea residents steered clear of lower Sloane Street. "At that hour the street was always filled with luxury cars taking children to Garden House," explained a local newsagent pointing to the entrance of one of London's most expensive private schools. "Kids don't just jump out of the car and dash inside; they expect the driver to open the door and help them out."

Private schools in England have always been "personalized." Some cater to gifted students, some educate the future wives of bankers, others teach children destined for military careers. Garden House is the school of the *nouveau riche*: people who have become billionaires courtesy of Mrs. Thatcher's privatization policies, the information technology (IT) revolution, or the collapse of the Soviet Union. In the early 1990s, globalization's superrich flocked en masse to London, creating a peculiar diaspora prompted by higher taxation at home. After 9/11, this influx peaked. People ran away from the new monetary controls imposed by the Patriot Act. From all corners of the global village, the well-to-do headed for their financial Promised Land.

Until the credit crunch, enrolling in schools like Garden House was not easy: demand far exceeded supply. A nonrefundable deposit secured the inclusion of future pupils among children who would be allowed to take the entrance test at age two and a quarter. But registration needed to be prompt. "When my husband and I visited Garden House's kindergarten, our twin daughters were three months old. We choose the school because it was right behind our house," remembered Francesca Mieli, a former economist at Goldman Sachs. "After visiting it, the director reproached us for being so late in applying; all available places had been already filled and the waiting list was full." A well-known, retired London obstetrician who delivered the heirs of the superrich at the luxurious, private Portland Hospital confirmed that, in a race to enroll fetuses in the best schools, his patients rang the school's admissions office as soon as they found out that they were pregnant.

The credit crunch has changed this scenario. Occupancy at the Portland is down 35 percent, and private care in general is also down. Many foreign nationals have been repatriated after losing their jobs in the city. Children have been taken out of private school because parents cannot afford the fees. The landscape is changing fast as the recession repaints it in dark, gloomy colors.

Garden House, Thomas's, and Newton Prep—schools frequented by the children of pop stars, artists, and designers—are all located in the most elite residential areas of central London: Chelsea, Kensington, Belgravia, and Knightsbridge. In the late 1970s and early '80s, Chelsea and Kensington—historically bohemian quarters where artists and musicians lived—became overrun with punk rockers. Eventually, the superrich of the global village kicked them out and gentrified these areas. The presence of so many well-to-do people pushed prices up. Until the fall of Lehman Brothers, everything in these rich neighborhoods was overpriced: in 2005, a 750-square-foot apartment cost the equivalent of more than $1 million, a coffee at Starbucks on King's Road sold for nearly five dollars, and dog hairstylist businesses charged seventy-five dollars to shampoo and style a pooch's 'do.

For over a decade, the trophy wives of the nouveau riche strolled the streets and visited the shops of these neighborhoods. "In the mornings they all wear designer tracksuits on their way to or back from exercise classes," attested Sola, an aesthetician at the exclusive Harbour Club of Fulham, where a private personal trainer used to earn up to $150 per hour. The superrich, however, do not frequent sports clubs. They exercise at home in their own gyms and swimming pools. Trainers, Pilates instructors, and yoga teachers regularly visit the mansions of the superrich. They charge more than $200 an hour for training and $300 for a shiatsu massage. Instructors, massage therapists, and aestheticians belong to a sort of caste of holistic servants that fulfill rich people's needs. The nouveau riche live an insular life and move exclusively inside a golden ghetto. "They abhor being in contact with common folks," explained Ellie, a now unemployed shampoo girl to a celebrity stylist. "When they come to the salon, they don't rub shoulders with other clients; we send them to private rooms."

At Asprey, a jeweler and luxury emporium on Bond Street, the superrich shop away from common people and from the disquieting nuisance of other shoppers. Almost all use a personal shopper, someone who assists them with important decisions: whether or not to match the new Asprey crocodile purse ($10,000) with a dyed cashmere jacket ($2,500), and whether this outfit could be improved with a finishing touch such as an art deco necklace of sapphires and diamonds ($35,000). "At times, I rushed to London to assist some client in a big dilemma about what to buy. This happens only when a new fashion designer is *en vogue*, a newcomer in the usual *haute couture* circuit. I know all collections by heart and can advise clients over the phone," explained Lawrence, a once sought-after personal shopper from New York who lost most of his clientele to the credit crunch.

Until the stock market crashed, the superrich—immortalized in Fay Weldon's *The Bulgari Collection*, a book commissioned by the famous jeweler himself—lived in a golden cage. Traveling by private jet, they were constantly surrounded by servants and assisted by chauffeurs, waiters, chefs, nannies, and butlers who organized their lives. "Without my chef and my chauffeur I would be lost," confessed a rich Londoner. "I can't even cook an egg and hardly know the streets of my area."

Based exclusively on their wealth and fame, in the 1990s, London's nouveau riche became known as celebrities. Joining the ranks of the Beckhams and pop singers like Oasis's Gallagher brothers were people made famous by their service to the superrich: jewelers, interior designers, famous chefs like Gordon Ramsay, and hairstylists like Nicky Clarke. At the lavish charity venues hosted at the Tate Modern, the superrich mingled with self-made tycoons such as Richard Branson, Rupert Murdoch, and Russian oligarch Roman Abramovich. After 9/11 this caste grew thanks to a large influx of people from Manhattan.

During this period, many intellectuals who had been prominent in the 1970s and '80s, symbols of Old London, felt compelled to move abroad. "I could no longer take the hedonistic political indifference of London during the reign of Blair's New Labour. Everything revolved around money, so I decided to move to Barcelona," declared Professor John Halliday. In high-society circles, New Labour politicians replaced intellectuals. New Labour's so-called "aspiring socialist" millionaires include the Blair couple, who purchased a $6 million home while residing at 10 Downing Street.

The superrich did not pay much attention to New Labour's failure to regenerate the city. Under Blair, London became one of the least livable and most dangerous cities in the world. In early 2000, it held the European record for car thefts and robberies. After 9/11, the city became the undisputed metropolitan icon of the West and Tony Blair the symbol of a new era. Few had the courage to point out this inconsistency, let alone mention that the emperor had no clothes. Among those few truth-tellers was Will Self, a prominent ex-Londoner and leftist writer. According to Self, Tony Blair's architectural heritage consists of the behemoth Millennium Dome, a now neglected structure that cost several billion pounds; the London Eye, a panoramic Ferris wheel chronically in the red; and a public transport system on the verge of collapse.

LONDON: TAX HAVEN OF THE NOUVEAU RICHE

The superrich did not settle in London for its beautiful architecture or the advantages of the Tube. They chose it because it is a tax haven. "The collapse of monetary and financial barriers allowed globalization's superrich to take advantages of an ancient Victorian law, using it to avoid taxation at home," explained Grant Woods, former director of Coutts, the bank of the British aristocracy and the royal family. "Created as an incentive to reinvest the profits earned by the British owners in the plantations of the West Indies, the law allowed them to maintain their residence in England while being domiciles abroad and to pay taxes only on what they spent or brought back to England." The same principle applied to the billionaires of globalization's moneyed diaspora, which explains why the largest number lives in London.

The Russians were the first superrich foreigners to settle in the capital, according to Woods. "While working at Coutts, I restructured the portfolio of several Russian oligarchs who took advantage of this law. Obtaining a residence permit was easy; all one had to do was deposit a large sum of money into an account and leave it there indefinitely." This was small change for someone who, by moving residence to London, could evade taxes on fortunes worth billions of dollars. Americans, however, could not take advantage of this law. "The US taxes its own citizens on global income, no matter where it is produced," informed Woods, explaining why relatively few superrich Americans reside in London.

The EU repeatedly exerted pressure on the Chancellor of the Exchequer to abolish this archaic law to be more in sync with the European fiscal system, but until the credit crunch, the English did not budge. "Harold Wilson, former Labour leader, wanted to abolish the law, but his government fell and nothing happened," Woods asserted. Before being elected, Gordon Brown promised such changes, but Blair had his mind set on something totally different: forging an alliance with the leaders of global finance to encourage them to conduct their business from London, paying as few taxes as possible. The attacks and aftermath of 9/11 helped Blair achieve this goal, as capital rushing out of the US was easily funneled to Britain. According to Woods, "the abolition of this law would produce a mass exodus of the superrich, who would search for yet another tax haven, the Channel Islands, Gibraltar, the Caribbean or Dubai, where life is certainly not at par with London's *dolce vita*." The new legislations discussed by the Group of Twenty (G-20) in 2009, to limit the ability of offshore facilities such as the Cayman Islands or Luxembourg to function as tax havens, do not include the abolition of the British Victorian law.

Irony of all ironies, Britain's economic dependence on this type of finance ended up turning against New Labour. According to the IMF and the Bank of England, Britain is the hardest hit of the major industrialized countries by the credit crunch, to the extent that it had to nationalize several banks and purchase 70 percent of many others. At the beginning of 2009, the projection for economic growth looked gloomy: a contraction of the economy by several percentage points, primarily due to the large role that the financial sector plays in the British GNP. In the spring of 2009, Standard & Poor's lowered its rating of the United Kingdom, fearing that the economy would not be able to service its debt.

PLAYING MONOPOLY IN THE GLOBAL VILLAGE

The events of 9/11 kick-started the exodus of globalization's moneyed elite from the US and transformed London into the Promised Land of the superrich. "The tough legislation passed in the US to halt money laundering and track down al-Qaeda's financiers—in other words, the Patriot Act—crippled the activities of the Caribbean tax havens. In addition, the US monetary authorities began monitoring dollar transactions globally. International banks did not like this supervision; that explains why the pound and the euro became the preferred currency of hedge funds, investment banks, and large investment funds—

organizations where the superrich stockpiled their profits," summarized Woods. After 9/11, these institutions set up shop in London.

A series of "friendly" laws reinforced the role of London as the financial center of the global village; among them was legislation that allowed trust funds to be tied to specific activities, often philanthropic, without proof of the origins of the fund. A London banker recalled that Mikhail Khodorkovsky, once Russia's wealthiest oligarch who was jailed on fraud charges in 2005, used this law to transfer over $500 million into an American bank in the city of London. According to then Russian President Vladimir Putin, the money stemmed from Khodorkovsky's Yukos Oil Company and violated Russian tax legislation. In other words, Khodorkovsky used the British law to evade taxes at home. Because the funds were placed in a trust to improve Russian education, they could not be touched, even after the former owner of Yukos was found guilty of tax evasion in Moscow. While nobody could withdraw the capital, it was possible to invest it and take the profits, and this is exactly what happened.

Against all odds, bin Laden turned London into the playground of globalization's nouveau riche, a phenomenon that greatly contributed to the expansion of the British financial bubble. Without 9/11, Blair's plan to move the center of global finance to London would never have come to fruition.

In the course of a few years, globalization's moneyed diaspora transformed London into a giant Monopoly game played by ultrarich couples. Around this game of Monopoly, so-called "artists" seemed to perpetually loiter: young graduates from Italian restoration schools hired as highly experienced professional decorators or interior designers, who accompanied their clients to art auctions; Asian architects with offices in New

York, Tokyo, and Shanghai; light sculptors commissioned to install fiber-optic ceilings. They too represented a sort of caste at the services of the superrich. The costs of these "professionals" were nauseating: £70,000 to paint a three-level staircase, £100,000 for a new kitchen. Like in the game of Monopoly, money circulated among players, financing a frenetic and extremely expensive race to stay abreast of the gazillion fashion trends of the moment.

In 2008, when the Lehman Brothers bankruptcy prompted the credit crunch, the game came abruptly to an end. London's booming real estate market crashed. "I had clients who every two years purchased a perfectly habitable mansion for £6, £7 million (over $10 million), hired architects, construction companies, and interior designers who demolished walls, ceilings, and floors. Then at the end of the remodeling they would say that the kitchen was too small, the bathrooms too dark, the street too loud, and they would start all over again," recalled a Belgravia realtor, currently unemployed. Naturally, mortgages funded these activities. The cost of money was so cheap that everybody, including the superrich, borrowed.

PART 2

THE FALL OF THE GLOBAL HOUSE OF CARDS

CHAPTER 9

THE BUBBLE BURSTS

SYMPTOMS OF THE NEW ECONOMIC MALAISE

When the bubble burst, there was no mistaking it. The US government's response to 9/11 spurred each element of a toxic mix—deflationary policy, risky new speculative markets, the draining off of Western dollars into Islamic banking, flourishing Islamic and European tax havens, and the repeal of key financial legislation. While 9/11 presented the circumstances under which these factors would devastatingly coalesce, individually, these factors largely dated back to the advent of globalization and the end of the cold war. This is particularly true of deflation.

Financial institutions took advantage of the low rates by refinancing loans or opening new accounts. Selling credit became a profit-making activity, and soon the world experienced the consequences of this policy: demand for real estate boomed. Anyone who did not already own a house bought one, and those who had one purchased a second.

Obviously, competition among banks for new customers was fierce and relentless. Some banks hired specialized brokers who worked in tandem with real estate agents, offering special incentives to anyone able to secure new contracts. As the demand for real estate escalated, competition became vicious as realtors demanded ever-greater margins to maneuver to attract new clients. Thus banks started to grant loans against less and less collateral.

After 9/11, the situation deteriorated. The Bush administration aggressively slashed interest rates, banks began to offer 100 percent mortgages, and the credit card sector planned a major expansionary move. As the financial sector offered consumer loans, often with ridiculously loose terms, herds of new clients flocked to request "plastic money." Banks even accepted certain credit cards, such as American Express Gold cards, as collateral for mortgages. Selling credit proved easy and profitable for banks, also thanks to the rising value of real estate. Higher housing prices ended up being used to raise banks' leverage, the ability to borrow, which in turn promoted banks' exposure to mortgages. Financial institutions borrowed against the increased value of the properties they were financing to buy mortgage-backed securities (MBS). These are real estate loans packaged together and transformed via derivatives into stocks or bonds. Their value is a function of the price of the real estate and of the interest rate. The more the former increases and the latter diminishes, the higher the value of the MBS.

From 2001 until 2007, when the subprime mortgage crisis erupted in the US, rising real estate prices and dropping interest rates inflated the value of MBSs. Only a relative few questioned why housing prices were going up or took into consideration the possibility that we lived inside a real estate bubble.

In order to expand the range of their clientele, banks started to sell risky subprime mortgages well below their traditionally accepted threshold. The global demand for MBS became so great that it would have seemed foolish not to produce more mortgages just because those applying for them didn't have enough income to pay. Of course, this was not a smart move, but at the time the risk of insolvency seemed super low because the interest rates kept plunging. Plus, a new type of mortgage loan on the market seemed to reduce this risk even further. These were the "interest only" loans in which, as the name states, only the interest was paid back without actually repaying the borrowed capital. The idea was that real estate prices would continue to go up forever and the principal would be paid back on the property's sale sometime before the loan reached maturity.

Retirement funds, hedge funds, and operators of the global village all coveted these American MBSs, gobbling them up. Thus real estate loans sold in Texas ended up in the retirement funds of Berlin dentists. All these investments were also driven by the profits expected from the increase in value of MBSs. Eventually, every increase in value led to an increase in debt to purchase further MBSs.

Interest rate cuts and the rise in real estate value produced fabulous profits for banks. In turn, they redistributed the money among shareholders and boards of directors. This explains the billions in bonuses, dividends, and compensation packages that engendered a whole new class of superrich within the bank sector. Profits, however, existed solely on paper: they were bookkeeping figures and represented the difference between the cost of the loan to be paid and the value of the goods that the loan purchased. When the latter decreased with the bubble burst, these proportions changed dramatically. The spectacular salaries that banks kept paying to their financial jockeys had depleted banks' reserves, their very *raison d'être*, in the absence of which a bank ceases to operate. This is why banks face a chronic shortage of cash in their vaults.

The global secondary market of the MBS turned out to be the curse of global finance. No link between MBS values and genuine economic growth existed; on the contrary, they depended on the ever-growing debt in the US and the world. When the latter reached an unsustainable level, defaults started. The inability of Americans to repay subprime mortgages triggered the crisis and then extended it like a tidal wave across all loans and markets.

The worst ramification of all this is that the money lost was ours. Banks used our deposits, our investments, our retirement funds, and our children's college funds to participate in the global village's game of Monopoly.

What tossed us into the abyss of the current recession is a mixture of ignorance and arrogance displayed by the "Masters of the Universe." Identical adjectives describe the popularity of the war on terror. It is precisely this parallel what we'll set out to analyze in the next chapter.

CHAPTER 10

THE POLITICS OF FEAR

THE ARROGANCE OF SIMPLETONS

The credit crunch is the latest chapter in the sad story of contemporary capitalism, a tale characterized by the arrogance and simplemindedness of its main protagonists, which became apparent while the entire world was concentrated on the threat posed by al-Qaeda. It seems absurd that an economic system powerful enough to cause revolutions and fratricidal wars, which has inspired whole generations and given life to one of the most potent ideologies of modern times, has disintegrated before our eyes because of the lies of its leaders and the lack of sophistication of its captains. The "Masters of the Universe" are really simpletons, people who have undermined the world economy for the sake of easy profits, thereby destroying the very system that supported them without even being aware of what they were doing. The politicians, too, are simpletons, making us believe that al-Qaeda was able to crush our world in order to pursue its hidden agenda when, in reality, those who were destroying it were prospering within it.

The financial sector that brought us to the credit crunch cannot, however, be defined as capitalism; Marx would be quick to point this out. It is rather a mix of political magicians, Monopoly players, and swindlers. True, authentic capitalism—that of the Industrial Revolution and the early 1900s—was an adversary worthy of respect, which exploited but neither stole nor swindled. It was also a shrewd and intelligent rival. This is the fundamental difference with the past: today those made rich by globalization are either thieves or simpletons.

However, we citizens of the global village, upon whom falls the tragic consequences of this crisis, also have behaved with arrogance and a lack of common sense. We have allowed the politicians to convince us to overextend ourselves in order to realize all our consumerist dreams: the house, the car, the vacations, the branded clothes and accessories, the high-tech gadgets, and more. This spending frenzy led us to believe that we were rich and powerful when, in reality, high finance was sucking our accounts dry and leaving us ever poorer. We acclaimed those who sold us these fantasies, the first and foremost of which was the fear of fundamentalist Islamic terrorism. How can we forget the popularity indices of Bush, Blair, José Maria Aznar, and Silvio Berlusconi when they incited the world to bomb Baghdad? Terrorized by the thought of losing our "place in the sun," we permitted the politics of fear to replace real politics and the act of governance to become a media event. We shouldn't be surprised when today we are called upon to pay the consequences.

THE ANATOMY OF THE COLD WAR

The world we live in is a labyrinth of fantasy, and politicians are the twenty-first century's great magicians, who sell fear and fabricate the truth. Among their greatest performances are

Saddam Hussein's weapons of mass destruction (WMDs) and Iraq's professed ability to launch a nuclear warhead that could strike Europe in forty-five minutes.

Political lies are incredibly potent, all the more so because these illusions seem to be more easily digested. The initial broad consensus in the West regarding the invasion of Iraq stemmed from the *a priori* certainty that what politicians tell us is the truth. It is this very point that requires analysis in order to properly understand why we ended up in this economic quagmire and, above all, how we can extricate ourselves.

In the case of Iraq, it seemed remarkable that so few felt compelled to pose some serious questions. First, if Saddam really had WMDs that could actually strike London, Paris, or Brussels within forty-five minutes, why was it that the spy satellites, which buzz around the planet like wasps, could not photograph them? Why had no one been able to provide the slightest shred of evidence to incontrovertibly support this alarming allegation? Moreover, if Saddam really had those weapons, why didn't he use them when he was attacked?

These are the questions that so few asked at the time. We all fell into the fantastical trap of the 007-style underground launch pads and the tanks laden with chemical weapons perpetually cruising the Iraqi highways. When it finally became clear that everybody had lied to us, we didn't have the courage to call to task the politicians who had sold us this pack of lies.

Politicians have always used a strategy of fear to achieve their goals and often have done so in a fashion very similar to that used by armed groups seeking to terrorize the population. Propaganda is the name of the game. Far from being a new phenomenon, the politics of fear is a traditional and highly effective instrument for gaining consensus, especially in the face of unpopular choices. Out of fear, we accepted as fact a series of unsubstantiated lies. Governments manipulated the apprehensiveness of their citizens in order to achieve their own political aims.

We should not feel singled out by history. This is certainly not the first time that politicians have manipulated public opinion. During the cold war, the United States built a nightmarish doomsday scenario around the specter of a potential victory by the Soviet enemy. This threat became the reference point upon which they leveraged a strategy of fear, a propaganda of fear that the US subsequently exported to Europe.

The Americans do it, and so do their adversaries. Within the Communist Bloc, the Soviet Union carried out a similar operation to maintain the status quo and safeguard its own survival, painting an image of the United States as a sinister power that would not hesitate to unleash another atomic bomb, thereby decimating hundreds of thousands of Russians and Eastern Europeans.

In reality, neither of the two superpowers had the slightest intention of using nuclear arms. The truth is that proliferation proved to be the best guarantee against nuclear tragedy. Confirmation of this can be seen in the way the two most serious nuclear crises of the postwar period—the tension leading to the erection of the Berlin Wall and the Cuban missile crisis— played themselves out. In both cases, the USA and the USSR used the impending nuclear menace as a means for consolidating their own spheres of influence, while taking great care to keep an appropriate distance from one another. The version sold to the general public is not this chronicle of a strategic battle carried out by cunning political chess players but rather the dramatic and anguished recounting of an event on the verge of the apocalypse.

The propaganda of fear has always been easily disseminated. Before the advent of the Internet, it traveled on the wings of documentaries and television spots—more basic and less widespread, but nonetheless more penetrating than the more ubiquitous Internet propaganda of today. During the 1960s, children watched short films produced by the US government, in particular by the Federal Civil Defense Administration, in which Bert the Turtle, a lively animated character, warned them that an atomic explosion could occur at any time without warning. "When you see the flash," said Bert with a sinister laugh, "you should duck down and find cover under the desk or in the school hallway." While Bert the Turtle pulled his head into his shell, the narrator's voice warned: "After the bomb explodes there might no longer be any adults around. Then you'll have to fend for yourselves." Politicians manufactured this equally scary nightmare for the youngest citizens, who would grow into adulthood with the constant perception of an enemy who, from one moment to the next, could turn their universe into dust.

Through the media, key political figures contributed to the spread of fear of a nuclear attack, especially in critical moments of heightened tension. In July 1961, during the Berlin Wall crisis, President John F. Kennedy gave a televised speech exhorting American families to build bomb shelters to "protect the nation." White House advertising was obviously employed skillfully in the marketing of these products; everyone rushed to buy their own bunker. In Prince George's County, Maryland, people did their "nuclear shopping"—already quite an unsettling activity— while listening to a male voice over the loudspeaker, exclaiming against a background of bombing and air-raid sirens: "My wife, my children . . . if I had only listened to the Civil Defense . . . now I'd be in the shelter." Sales grew exponentially.

Among the pillars of the cold war one finds fear of a nuclear attack, just as the fear of a terrorist nuclear attack became the *leitmotif* of Bush's war on terror. Right after 9/11, Washington dusted off the potent and terrifying image of the atomic mushroom cloud rising over a Western city. Not coincidentally, the most common motivation used to justify the war in Iraq rested on the danger posed by weapons of mass destruction. History tends to repeat itself even in its least virtuous chapters. Just as before, this fear is based on false information. The politicians know it; we don't.

Only now do we have at our disposal the information confirming that Saddam Hussein no longer had weapons of mass destruction, much less the intention to sell them to al-Qaeda. The Iraqi president pretended to possess a nuclear program, partly to support his megalomaniac propaganda machine and partly to scare off Iran. In his distorted vision, he believed he could keep his enemies at bay with these lies.

If it is indeed true that the CIA, the Pentagon, and the European secret services did not know his strategy, then one should wonder whether these organizations are at all capable of doing their work. Many people have their doubts, although few have the courage to admit it. And still fewer people ask themselves another question: is it true that even in the absence of Saddam Hussein a nuclear attack by some armed group is still possible? The politicians and the media would have us believe that the answer is yes.

In 2006, when it became apparent that Saddam did not have nuclear weapons, Peter Zimmermann and Jeffrey Lewis wrote—in "The Bomb in the Backyard," an article published in the journal *Foreign Policy*, complete with a hypothetical model of a clandestine nuclear complex—that bin Laden could have attacked the US with an atomic bomb built secretly in a minicomplex in the style of Los Alamos in the United States. No one questioned this absurd scenario! Any nuclear technology expert could have done so. It would have sufficed to mention just one obstacle: even supposing that the terrorists had been able to get their hands on the uranium and plutonium required to produce the bomb, they would have needed to be enriched to bomb grade, an operation alone that would have required energy sufficient to black out the entire northeastern United States.

We need to ask ourselves these questions: why do the media continue to transmit apocalyptic messages, and why do we continue to believe them? Perhaps that is the same explanation for why there was no questioning or doubting of the chilling declarations by politicians in the aftermath of 9/11. Though the media's and the politicians' common interests in the construction of catastrophic scenarios rest on the fact that what frightens us also draws our attention, clearly increasing media audiences and newspaper sales, what is harder to explain is the public's lack of skepticism. Why did we believe everything we were told? Why did so few ask why, if it was so easy to get hold of nuclear weapons, has not one terrorist done it yet?

THE DANGER BEHIND THE FEAR OF TERRORISM

The illusions created to terrorize us don't end here. Even the belief that Westerners are more exposed than ever to the risk of terrorism relies on a series of falsehoods: data demonstrate that, in the West, the armed struggle reached its apex in the late 1970s and early '80s and has been in decline ever since. Even taking into account 9/11, Westerners have a higher risk of being hit by lightning than of dying in a terrorist attack.

In the Muslim world, we find a different scenario. Since 9/11, violence has risen. MIPT-RAND, considered the most reliable data bank on terrorism, confirms that the number of attacks in the region defined as the Middle East/Persian Gulf rose from fifty prior to 9/11 to 4,800 in the year 2006. In the same period, deaths from terrorism in the region soared from less than a hundred to 9,800.

Therefore, the real primary victim of terrorism is the Muslim world, that which we believe poses a threat, the world the Crusades destroyed. The invasion of Iraq marks an important watershed because, instead of slowing terrorist activity in the region, the invasion fed it. "The Iraq Effect"—a study of the consequences of the war, published in 2006 in *Mother Jones* magazine—shows that since the official beginning of the war in 2003, the incidence of terrorist attacks and the average level of consequent deaths on a global scale increased by 607 and 237 percent respectively.

Therefore, death at the hands of terrorists is always found more in areas far from the West, and in Iraq the death toll has reached shocking levels. According to the respected British medical journal the *Lancet*, in the first two years of the war over 100,000 perished—more than the combined worldwide total of victims of terrorism during the entire twentieth century.

It is perhaps worthwhile to stop for a moment to analyze the intellectual arrogance and indifference of Westerners when it comes to the tragedy befalling certain Muslim countries. Few of us are concerned about what happens outside the confines of our own worlds. Why should we be surprised? These have been years of great plenty, of a collective inebriation during which we have passed the time spending money we didn't have while all around us wars were raging. Now that the money has run out, we have become forcibly aware of our mistakes. In the global village, we no longer have the luxury of ignoring anything because we are all part of the same economy.

Herein lies the deep contradiction of modern politics: these are leaders who, on one hand, frighten us to death and who, on the other hand, sell us the ephemeral illusion of a wealth that does not exist, exhorting us to spend and enjoy what we do not possess.

What if the lack of critical thought with which we accepted the post-9/11 multiple apocalyptic scenarios—what if the real root of our fear—is not the fear of dying in a terrorist attack but rather the idea of losing our comfort, our well-being, the wealth accumulated since the fall of the Berlin Wall? This is an uncomfortable question we should ask ourselves.

The fact remains, however, that we are scared and that Westerners feel more exposed to the risks of terrorism today than in the past. How can one still be shocked when one has viewed history's most devastating and globally unifying reality show? Watching the destruction of the twin towers on live TV profoundly damaged our subconscious. Thanks to CNN and other networks that brought the tragedy in real time to the four corners of the globe, the fear became immediate, shared, and planetary. From Beijing to São Paulo, from Rome to Reykjavik, we all felt personally involved.

Even though nobody could deny that those distressing images forced us to confront the tragic consequences of terrorism, it is equally true that the media emphasis and manipulation of the events have so shaken our sensitivities as to cause us to internalize the fear of terrorism, transforming an exceptional and extraordinary event into a daily anxiety.

Once more, let us try to stop, take a deep breath, recover our rationality, and ask ourselves: What are we really scared of? Of dying like the victims of 9/11 or of losing, at the hands of this frightening enemy, the primacy that we have maintained over the world for centuries? What scares us more: the spectacular terrorist act or the rhetoric of the clash of civilizations?

If our sincere response is adherence to Samuel Huntington's theory of the clash of civilizations, then the political magicians have done a good job and we are doubly naïve; the events of the last eight years confirm it. This is exactly what we have been trying to understand from the beginning of this book. The destruction of the primacy of the richest economies has not come at the hands of Osama bin Laden but rather as a result of our ignorance, our superficiality, our greed—traits we share with globalized finance—and, of course, the arrogance of those who govern us.

So here, in sum, is how we ended up in this trap: For the average inhabitant of the global village, the internalization of terrorism took place when it ceased to be regarded as a crime and became a form of total war against one's way of life. The conflict, not the exceptional criminal event, puts one's life at risk. There is nothing as terrifying as war, and nothing frightens us more than an adversary who looks different from us. After 9/11, the absurd theory of the clash of civilizations re-invoked memories of the racial violence of the Holocaust. This time the enemy is Muslim but the objective is still genocide. We hear again the most terrifying mantra of all: they hate us because we are not like them. Difference, not politics, is the main source of fear generated by Islamic terrorism.

With great skill, politicians and the media built a politics of fear around this psychosis, presenting al-Qaeda as the new Nazi movement and Osama bin Laden as the reincarnation of Adolf Hitler. This was enough to convince the population that the survival of Western culture was again at risk. And all this while the ones who were really chipping away, destroying piece by piece our world and our well-being, were neither living in the tribal regions of Pakistan nor were dressed in rags, but rather were living on Wall Street and in the city of London.

Wearing bespoke pin-striped suits and flying in their private jets, the destroyers of modern capitalism were flattered by the politicians and acclaimed by the media.

THE INDUSTRY OF TERRORISM

Another unsettling reality to emerge from this situation is that we know so little about what has really happened. No one has tried to tell us that, before 9/11, al-Qaeda was a little organization rife with internal fighting, completely absent from the West and its message unknown to the world. Why has it been hidden from us that the majority of its members did not share the racial and religious hatred bin Laden felt toward America?

Constructing a series of lies and dressing them up with a mythology of terrorism has been relatively easy because, until 9/11, this phenomenon had been practically unknown. Until that moment, a bibliographic search of the term "terrorism" would have turned up a mere handful of titles, essays, and articles; today, there are thousands.

Until 2001, the international community of experts on terrorism was very small and the academic community smaller still; no university offered any degree courses on this topic. Overall, there were but a handful of private security agencies handling the phenomenon. In the US, for example, there were only five, while today there are more than 40,000.

The politics of fear has been good business for those in a position to take economic advantage of its spread. The industry of fear, fed and maintained by new apocalyptic stories, was quick to prosper. But we must not forget the accomplices of the political classes: the ranks of experts, consultants, professors, and, alas, even charlatans, who have supplied the fuel to create a gigantic bonfire.

The Internet has shown itself to be the principal means of propaganda. There are thousands of consulting companies that exist solely online. After 9/11, with expert groups at conferences, academics, contractors, newspapers, blogs, terrorist websites, and more offering information on what there is to know and do to prevent terrorist attacks, online services became the heart of a flourishing sector. Terrorism experts, sprouting like mushrooms after a rain, confirmed the gloomiest declarations of the leaders and the apocalyptic scenarios painted on TV and radio, manipulating data to provide proof of the strengthening of armed organizations and publishing reports online.

The statistics and false information satisfied the media's unquenchable thirst for "frightening news." The politicians altered the facts, uttering inflated truths and sometimes out and out lies. The media broadcasted them. We got upset, starting to fear anyone who had features, dress, and customs different from ours. Yet it never occurred to us to pay attention to what was happening on Wall Street, where it was said that they were making money by the bucket load. On the contrary, we did everything we could to scrape up a few crumbs ourselves from that treasure trove, and it never entered our minds that it was there that our peace and our system of values were suffering the most threatening attack.

The likelihood that bin Laden will destroy us is extremely low; the likelihood that finance will do so is, on the other hand, extremely high, a virtual certainty.

CHAPTER 11

LAS VEGAS AND DUBAI: "MIRROR, MIRROR, ON THE WALL, WHO'S THE RICHEST OF THEM ALL?"

GAMBLING WHILE VACATIONING WITH HIGH FINANCE

Some of the money sent from Dubai to the 9/11 hijackers ended up in Las Vegas. According to FBI documents, some of the members of the al-Qaeda suicide squad made repeated visits to the city before the attacks. These trips to "the Coney Island for adults" remain one of the unsolved riddles of the preparatory phases of 9/11. Just as it seems impossible to trace the account holders of the money sent from Dubai to Mohamed Atta and his fellow hijackers, no one seems able to establish what the loyal followers of Osama bin Laden were doing in the "Vice Capital of the World."

This double mystery is but one of the many ties that link two desert cities on opposite sides of the world. The analogies don't end here: Both cities represent the plastic vision of over a decade of uninterrupted economic growth, produced when the real estate financial bubble started to inflate. Las Vegas became the global village's capital of legal gambling and Dubai, an important center of globalized finance, morphed into the most dynamic tax haven east of the United Kingdom.

Until the middle of 2008, Las Vegas registered the fastest population growth in the United States, to the point that the city opened a new school every month. Every year a noisy stream of tens of millions of visitors flocked to the Strip, that asphalt belt studded with the neon lights of casinos and gigantic fashionable hotels, which, from the sky, resembles a multicolored landing strip in the middle of the Nevada desert. This capital of kitsch, with its replica Eiffel Tower and even a hotel reconstruction of Venice, reached its maximum hotel capacity of 150,000 rooms only at the beginning of 2008. Even though new hotels sprang up like mushrooms throughout Vegas, for years the city had operated at nearly full occupancy.

Tourism and real estate fuel the Vegas economy, but the real engine of the system is gambling. Equally, Dubai has made tourism and real estate the levers of its growth while the commercial heart of the city continues to be finance, where the gambling risk is not very different from that at the green felt tables.

In the United States, the passion for gambling exploded at the end of the 1980s, exactly when the process of globalization was about to take off. Until that moment, it was legal to gamble only in two states. But in the space of less than a decade, the situation has evolved to the point that today the picture is completely reversed: gambling is legal in forty-eight states while only Utah and Hawaii prohibit this activity. The numbers are impressive: every year almost 160 million Americans gamble in casinos, compared to a total of 177 million who attend baseball, football, hockey, and basketball games.

Gambling has become the most popular entertainment industry in America, employing around half a million people, more than half of whom live in Las Vegas. It is certainly not a coincidence that in the last fifteen years this industry's growth has kept in lockstep with that of the financial industry. It is certainly not surprising, seeing as these activities are substantially similar, both exploiting the many sides of risk.

The advent of multimillion-dollar bonuses came in the early 1990s; since then, several zeros have been added to them. In other words, their growth has been exponential. In tandem, gambling industry profits have soared: in 1995 they were $45 million in the United States; by 2004 they had doubled and, once again, 40 percent of them originated in Las Vegas.

Until the credit crunch, Las Vegas, like Dubai, was seen primarily as a vacation city, a place where people purchase second or third homes and where buying property has become a popular form of investment. In these cities, where people can become owners in a matter of days, the housing buy-sell race reached its apex. As a consequence, the city hosted a large number of subprime mortgages, those granted to people who had serious problems honoring their financial commitments.

Thanks to the policy of low interest rates, for the last fifteen years buying property in Las Vegas had been within almost everyone's grasp. But the real booming years started after 9/11 when the Fed slashed interest rates, which bottomed around 1.5 percent. In the golden years from 2002 to 2006, real estate agents turned customers onto mortgages exceeding 100 percent of the property value. To qualify for them, borrowers only had to be employed—any old job would do. The aggressively low interest rates coupled with strong demand for houses set off fierce competition among real estate agents and banks to secure new clients. An identical phenomenon took place in Dubai, where property companies worked in tandem with banks to offer potential buyers "full service" at rock-bottom prices.

The demand proved plentiful. Until 2007, 6,000 to 7,000 people per month moved to Las Vegas. Many, after only a few weeks, bought houses and settled permanently in the city. Few had problems finding work, and the unemployment rate was among the lowest in America.

Similarly, Dubai grew up in the space of a few decades. In the 1990s, this outcropping of the Arabian desert with a tiny port transformed itself into a modern city. But it was during the property boom, between 2002 and 2008, that this emirate began to resemble an international megalopolis. Finance professionals moved to Dubai, from where they managed mostly Eastern portfolios. They lived and worked in skyscrapers built on desert sand, soon to become symbols of the new world.

Constantly lit like daylight, Dubai and its American twin sister never slept. "Money doesn't rest," says Gordon Gekko in the film *Wall Street*; it is this mantra that the inhabitants of the artificial desert metropolis have made their own.

MONEY, MONEY, MONEY

Just as gambling represents the economic heart of Las Vegas, so the game of finance was the heart of Dubai. But even if Islamic finance constructed a large international business hub in the city, Dubai grew mainly because it was a tax haven, therefore attracting a particular type of investor.

First there were the Pakistanis, followed closely by the Indians and the Russians, who considered the emirates the "Florida of the East." In the winter months, airlines shuttled hordes of Russians to and from Moscow and Dubai.

The emirate also became an important hub for the trade— and contraband—of gold. In 2001, the United Nations began a series of investigations into its role in the smuggling of Congolese gold coming out of Uganda. This trade violated the UN-imposed sanctions on the Congo.

Until its financial collapse, millionaire tourism and murky businesses, such as money laundering, seemed to be the main sources of wealth for Dubai, with its permissive legislation. Limited customs controls transformed this artificial metropolis into an ideal location to launder the ill-gotten gains of criminal activity. The Asian mafias quickly recognized it and established important bases in the emirate.

However, the image that Dubai projected to the world until recently seemed quite different. Like Las Vegas, Dubai was perceived as a sophisticated amusement park for adults, a sort of adults' Disneyland of globalization. The offer of entertainment attracted the conventionally globalized individuals who went to Dubai on vacation to sate their curiosity.

Behind this illusion one finds a precise and deliberate marketing strategy. Unlike the other emirates, Dubai has few oil reserves, a relative handicap it overcame by encouraging its tourism and finance sectors. This formula grew on the back of the murky businesses, such as money laundering, and produced an economic boom exceeding even the most optimistic projections. Then the bubble burst, and everything changed.

That tourism is a cyclical industry will surprise no one. The problem is that both Las Vegas and Dubai really possess very little else. For Dubai, the long wave of the financial crisis brought a contraction of the easy-money industry and the city went almost instantly into recession, then eventually went broke. The decline in gambling brought on by the recession also proved fatal for Las Vegas. Once boasting full employment and work for all, today the world's capital of vice ranks among cities with the highest unemployment rates.

On opposite sides of the world, the shining skyscrapers in

the desert are becoming ever emptier. In Las Vegas, apartment sales have declined from one hundred to one per month, and although Dubai avoids disclosing this type of statistic, everyone knows that the property sector in the emirate is collapsing. Russian buyers, who represented a critical mass of buyers, are nowhere to be found. Other Western vacation communities keep disappearing along with the rich Russians. Fabulous villas and luxury apartments built on the new artificial islands remain empty and unsold. A long strip of dark and empty monsters, with only the occasional eerie and sinister light shining through, runs parallel to the Las Vegas strip, still lit by casinos and the spectacular neon lights of hotels with increasing vacancies. In Dubai, too, empty skyscrapers look out like gigantic ghosts of a shining past over landscapes of cement and sand running toward the sea. The legendary malls of the emirate, giant commercial centers where people could visit one of the world's largest aquariums or even ski, today look half empty. The casinos and bars of Las Vegas aren't faring so well either.

In the summer of 2008, Las Vegas led the nation in foreclosures. Many people abandoned their homes just as soon as their values fell below that of the mortgage amount outstanding. What sense does it make to continue to pay for a house, making an enormous sacrifice, knowing that it represents a loss? Better to pack your bags and seek your fortune elsewhere. But where? Las Vegas and Dubai were among the first victims of the recession but by no means are they the only ones.

All across America unemployment is spreading like a virus. Soon the desolation that characterizes these cities will become ubiquitous. As a natural consequence, the social fabric of the two cities is crumbling. The suicide rate in southern Nevada is twice the national rate. Las Vegas also has the highest number of school dropouts and the most residents not covered by health insurance.

In Dubai, an army of foreign workers and laborers have already lost their jobs; four-fifths of the population of the megalopolis is made up of foreigners. Indian workers alone number 1.5 million in the emirate, some of whom live on the streets without sufficient money to pay for lodging, much less for a plane ticket home.

Michael Green, professor of history at the University of Southern Nevada and a Las Vegas resident, defines the recession as that element which demolishes the illusion of wealth. It seems right to apply this phrase to the global village because illusion is what characterizes it. For years, just as those who failed in New York, Washington, and Chicago packed their bags and traveled to Nevada to try their luck there, in the same way the poor of the East made their way to Dubai to seek their fortunes. In both cases, however, very few have become wealthy. Today their fates seem tied, in a double-edged way, to that of the city in which they reside.

ELVIS'S BROTHER

Anything is possible in the fantasy universe populated by the illusions of years of fake wealth. The story of Jesse Grice in Las Vegas reads like a parody of the rise and fall of America's adult Disneyland.

Jesse was twenty-seven years old in 1993 when he arrived in Las Vegas in the midst of a great metamorphosis. From a smallish city of a few hundred thousand inhabitants with a single strip, it soon turned into the entertainment mecca of the global village. A generation of hoteliers and business visionaries invested tens of billions of dollars, much in the manner of

Bugsy Siegel, the legendary gangster who founded Vegas in the early 1900s. They clearly sensed that globalization had unleashed an insatiable demand for entertainment and legitimated an unrestrained and ostentatious display of wealth. Slowly but surely, the city became the distorting mirror of the new world. Despite the explosion of theme hotels, none represented the dream, the flight from reality. Rather, they celebrated a "plastic" vision of the world in which we live: reborn in the sands of the Nevada desert stood Venice alongside Paris, New York, even the pyramids of Egypt. The key phases of world history appeared along the strip, like the cardinal points of a new compass whose magnetic north is money.

For almost two decades, the real world mirrored the city's grand illusion as Las Vegas celebrated the dream of unlimited wealth. Tourists flocked to it, loving the idea of burning wealth at the gaming tables.

The entertainment industry soon came within reach of wallets of any size, from the ten-dollar hookers at the edge of the strip to the nouveau riche frequenting ultra-luxurious casinos; from the spectacular shows of Cirque du Soleil to the fashion shows at the Atrium Suites Hotel; from replicas of famous monuments like the Statue of Liberty to the twenty-four-hour strip joints.

Jesse quickly realized that no one had thought much about the rich market of Elvis fans: in all of Las Vegas he could not find one impersonator, not a single show dedicated to the great singer. He had a brilliant idea: in order to keep some distance from the banality of the classic impersonator, he assumed the identity of Elvis's stillborn brother, Jesse Garon. He recreated the dream of a generation through Elvis's bloodline. Jesse Garon is not Elvis, but he is about as close as one can get on this earth to an encounter with the deceased legend.

Within a short time, Jesse became an attraction. The casinos and the "in" bars called him to do shows and he even ended up on the cover of *Time* magazine. A river of money started to flow, and Jesse built a ranch outside the city, which he designed, incredibly, as a copy of Graceland. The expenses were stratospheric, the mortgage almost prohibitive; the property was really beyond Jesse's means. But these were the years of easy credit and a good market, the years of the miracle of wealth, and so it was possible to find a bank ready to front him a bundle of money.

Who could imagine that a money machine like Las Vegas, which for more than fifteen years had worked perfectly, would one fine day break down? In 2002, 50 million people visited the city; in 2004, the total rose by 5 million. This figure represents around 40 percent of the adult population of America. The average gambling time is around five hours, and each player "spends"—a euphemism for "loses"—on average $500 a day. The math is easy. A single slot machine takes in $250,000 per day, and there are hundreds of thousands in Vegas.

These statistics give the impression of absolute wealth, of an empire ready to withstand any onslaught. Nothing could be further from the truth. It didn't take much to dim the ephemeral light projected by these numbers and throw the city into recession.

In a short space of time, Jesse, too, lost his ranch, his contracts, and his fans. As the recession's vengeance spread like an oil slick, people no longer wanted to dream to the sound of the King's songs. The Las Vegas parabola began its declining phase.

THE MIRRORS OF OUR WORLD

One critical look at what has happened to the two desert metropolises, separated by thousands of miles of ocean and land, and one understands that their intertwined destinies have nothing to do with the recession and the real life disasters it visits. Rather, Las Vegas and Dubai are two poles of the globalized world, symbols of a planet that has lost its social and existential compass and that, at least for the last decade, has been drifting in a sea of illusions.

The two cities find themselves mysteriously interconnected even by the tragedy of 9/11: the hijackers visited Las Vegas several times, and many believe that they planned their suicidal attacks from this city. Some of the money they spent in Vegas had been transfered from secret accounts in Dubai.

The shimmering metropolis of Nevada became the symbol *par excellence* of the vice and weakness of the West, at the center of harsh criticism by Sayyid Qutb, one of the spiritual leaders of jihadism.

Qutb is the Egyptian intellectual who founded the Muslim Brotherhood, and his radical theses constitute the basis of al-Qaeda's creed of violence. After having traveled in America for much of 1949, Qutb described it on his return to the homeland as a decadent and, at the same time, primitive society: decadent because it is consumerist and lacking in real ideals, primitive because it is slave to sexual desire.

No American city better embodies the erosion of values and the disquieting sense of decline of traditions and customs than Las Vegas. But Western analysts misinterpreted the hijackers' trip to the city.

The official interpretation relates that the funds that left Dubai ended up in an orgy of vice to which the terrorists abandoned themselves before their suicide operation. This is highly unlikely. Radical religious Muslims regarded Dubai as the capital of vice within the Islamic world: people drank alcohol and went to discos, men and women danced in close proximity while from the minarets of the mosques the sounds of the *muezzin* resonated.

We will probably never know who in Dubai sent the money to 9/11 hijacker Mohamed Atta and his companions, nor why they went to Las Vegas; on the subject we can offer little more than conjecture. Ultimately, the unraveling of this mystery is not that important, given that it will not shed much light on our understanding of how terrorism and the economic crisis have become so intertwined as to merge themselves into two faces of the same coin.

It is far more important to understand what fuelled the exponential growth of these two monumental metropolises, cities that celebrate the symbols of the globalized, out-of-control economy. At the root of this process one finds the very same frenzy, the neurotic daily rat race that also characterizes high finance—the insatiable thirst for money. It is the same anguished lust for power of the neoconservatives, so determined to remove Saddam Hussein from power at all costs and to redesign the power map of the Middle East, under the aegis of the American eagle.

The financial wizards, political magicians, and con artists who represent us all seem prey to the same unmanageable existential insecurity. They always want and seek more; they want it all and are consumed by the fear of failure. They seem obsessed with the possibility that in the crazy race someone might do better than them. A rat race it is: Dubai built the tallest skyscraper in the world, a vertical kilometer of cement; Las Vegas brought gondolas to the desert; and the sky seemed to be the limit for Wall Street's Dow Jones. One cannot avoid thinking that they all resemble the stepmother of Snow White, standing in front of the mirror obsessively demanding: "Mirror, mirror, on the wall, who is the fairest of them all?"

This mantra reveals the true values of Western society: those with more money and power are those who really count. The 9/11 attackers went repeatedly to Las Vegas to hear that mantra; drunk on the jihadi doctrine, they wanted to touch with their own hands the capitalist cancer that threatened to spread east and that had already infected Dubai. So we return to the purifying role of the suicidal attacks in the collective imagination of al-Qaeda.

The effect of the economic crisis on these cities seems to support these hypotheses. The invisible thread that we have followed from the beginning of this book, which links Dubai to 9/11, was not severed when the planes crashed on American soil; instead it continued to strengthen and today ties the two poles of the global village, symbols of the ephemeral triumph of globalization—Las Vegas and Dubai—to the misfortune of recession.

These two metropolises built on sand, now more than anything, represent the mirrors of our world. Through them we can visualize our mistakes. They project images of the crazy race to ethereal wealth, a goal that blinded us to the point of rendering us insensitive to the true needs of society, of forgetting the values upon which we have built free and democratic nations. Not only this. It is this crazy race toward the ephemeral—disguised as an absolute certainty—that prevented us from clearly seeing the enormous meteorite that crashed down upon us.

Las Vegas and Dubai are no longer the magical mirrors that projected the "world beyond reality" where we lived until just yesterday, a world that is now breaking into pieces, presaging seven years of scarcity. The reality is in the distorted and unseemly images that emerge from the fragments. They reflect the embarrassing ingenuousness with which we fell prey to two gigantic mystifications: on the one hand, the strategy of fear administered by the politicians; on the other, the irresistible fascination with the fatuous promise of eternal wealth with which the financial class enticed us.

CHAPTER 12

THE DANGER OF PROTECTIONISM

THE ECONOMIC CRISIS OF THE 1930s

Globalized finance transformed the invisible hand of Adam Smith into the prestidigitation of a magician. The credit crunch woke us all up from a dream, and now we see that a large part of the wealth accumulated in the 1990s and 2000s was only a mirage. This illusion spread universally because fear of terrorism absorbed all our attention and energies. Not for one instant did we doubt that bin Laden had the means to destroy our "place in the sun," and such fear became so strong and real that we paid no attention to the systematic theft of our savings at the hands of high finance. In the words of President Franklin Delano Roosevelt, "the only thing we have to fear is fear itself." Like the characters in *The Wizard of Oz*, we lived in fear of a peril that did not exist, something that was only a figment of our imagination. This paranoia grew while the wizards of Wall Street emptied our bank accounts. As in the Hollywood masterpiece, so too is in real life: the shocking revelations keep coming. Around the corner lurks the specter of protectionism, which could wipe away what little wealth we still possess. This time we must keep our eyes open and resist being manipulated by the magic tricks of politicians.

Ever since the credit crunch turned into a global recession, another capitalist economic principle has come under attack: free trade. "By specializing in the production of some products instead of pursuing self-sufficiency," wrote Adam Smith, "each nation derives benefit from international exchange." Economist David Ricardo echoed Smith when he differentiated—thanks to the concept of comparative advantage—among goods to be produced at home, those to be exchanged, and merchandise to be imported. For centuries these postulates represented the pillars of modern economics and they continue to do so, despite routinely being put under pressure each time the world is shaken by yet another economic crisis.

The problem springs from the inability of governments to manage periods of wealth contraction. A successful counter-cyclical policy or an antirecession strategy do not exist. Modern politicians can sell anything to the population—they even convinced the world that Saddam Hussein had weapons of mass destruction—but they cannot make people accept that the economy resembles a roller coaster that goes up and down, often unexpectedly. This is despite the fact that economic history and theory teach us that inflation, recession, and even stagnation and depression belong to the economic cycle, just as much as growth and prosperity. Therefore, each and every time things don't go as expected, when growth slows down, politics seeks to rewrite the economic theory; and the common knee-jerk reaction to an economy in recession becomes protectionism. The simplest and most efficient strategy for making people believe that the responsibility for the crisis lies with other nations, protectionism is also synonymous with nationalism. It is the Joker that can be played at the moment of the game's most serious difficulty. Americans, Europeans, Asians, anybody who loses his job or her home wants to be reassured that if the government can't promise them employment, at least it will commit to not giving a job to a foreigner! This might explain the motive for the recent unhappy phrase that Gordon Brown uttered in the midst of the crisis: "British jobs to British citizens."

Everyone recognizes the danger inherent in the protectionist lexicon—a sort of populist economics—yet we are willing to take such risk to appease, in the short run, any opposition and silence any criticism. Protectionism has never helped anyone; on the contrary it hurts those who pursue it. The depression of the 1930s acquired the epithet "great" when it became a protectionist struggle between nations. Since the beginning of the 1920s, this wind shook the US, but it became a virtual hurricane only in 1930 with the approval of the Smoot-Hawley Tariff Act, sponsored by the unpopular President Herbert Hoover. The act inflicted the coup de grâce on free trade, which had shrunk to 40 percent of its 1929 figure by 1934. It is unquestionable that the law deepened the depression. American exports declined from $2.3 billion in 1929 to barely $784 million in 1933. Far from resolving unemployment, the legislation worsened it; the unemployment rate jumped from 7.8 percent in 1930 to 25 percent in 1933.

THE MANTRA OF PROTECTIONISM

Sadly, in the world of economics and politics, historical amnesia has become widespread. Barack Obama may commit the same errors Herbert Hoover made when he proposes economic rescue plans conditioned upon the purchase of Made in America products, such as metal and steel. Buy American, the new political mantra, recalls the mantra of old launched by President James Monroe, "America for the Americans." Today the United States has responsibilities toward the rest of the planet, not only because among the principal causes of this crisis one finds its celebrated banking system—exported just about everywhere in the world after the fall of the Berlin Wall—but also and especially because, since World War II, this great nation has assumed leadership of the world's economy.

Nevertheless, who could resist the protectionist mantra? Similar to a miraculous prayer, it quiets, at least temporarily, the fears coursing through civilian society. The global village is terrorized indeed. The politics of fear of the Bush years have disproportionately inflated the threat of those reputed "aliens," "different" from us. Foreign culture, religion, and ideology represent the roots of the clash of civilizations. But embracing protectionist propaganda only perpetuates this ill-conceived and false notion. Just as the war on terror has not pacified the world—indeed it has made it more violent and has contributed to the recession—so too the raising of tariff barriers or the "Buy American" mantra will make economic recovery harder.

Protectionism resembles a virus similar to the one unleashed by the fear instilled by al-Qaeda—once exposed to the light of day it becomes difficult to stop it from spreading. But the infection represents only the surface of the damage that protectionism causes to society; an even more worrying disability is the rising tide of intolerance toward those who are different from us.

FEAR OF THOSE WHO ARE DIFFERENT FROM US

The globalized planet is a world that scares its inhabitants, a planet populated by people terrorized by differences and by "those who are not like us." In a nutshell, this is the existential inheritance that the neoconservative hawks left us. We realize it only now that the recession has become our common misfortune, but it has been the case for the last twenty years that those who exist at the margins of the global village—where globalization's process of homogenization has not brought peace and prosperity but has instead fomented wars and deepened poverty—have been living in fear. Many, especially the young, have sought protection by replicating the tribal structure of the gangs.

From the Mara Salvatrucha gang members of Central America to the urban gangs of the UK, from the bands of young Nigerians to the jihadist cells, the gang has become the vehicle to fend off globalization's fear and menace. The common matrix of the new tribalism is violence. Just as in the past, today gangs fight fear with violence, and, in the end, violence becomes a type of lifestyle.

Fear of those "alien" to us has been creeping around the global village for a long time and has penetrated the lexicon of terrorism, and more recently provided the building blocks for the language of the war on terror. The politics of fear carried out by the Bush administration even catapulted such paranoia into the international political arena. In Bush's famous speech just after 9/11, he divided the world into two groups—"those who are with us and those who are against us"—a sentence that the British newspaper the *Guardian* has described as "the crudest expression of tribal politics ever conceived." How can we define them and us if, for example, the London suicide attackers were British citizens? Nationality, the basis for old-fashioned nationalism, not only is no longer the sole determinant of the individual, it may no longer be a valid category. Tribalism appears to better represent the social co-location of men and women in the global-ized village.

Even without knowing it, we assimilate the tribal lexicon, and when we feel threatened, our tribal instincts motivate our reactions. Racism, xenophobia, protectionism: these similar expressions well describe our world. The most chilling consequence of the folly that became the war on terror is the paranoid ranting about al-Qaeda and Saddam Hussein that took place while the wizards of Wall Street gambled away the shirts on our backs: reduced to behaving like a pack of rabid animals, consumed by anger and wolfish aggression toward others who are different from us yet equally victims of tribalism.

These are frightening scenarios that should make us reflect on the true perils of a planet in the throes of recession and sliding toward protectionism. A little less than a century ago, the crash of Wall Street plunged the world into the Great Depression, prelude to the Nazi folly, which culminated in World War II. Even then what drove the rise of Nazism from the ashes of the Weimar Republic was the fear of those who were different from us—men, women, and children forced to wear a yellow Star of David on their breasts. In Italy and many other countries that fell victim to fascism, those regarded as "alien" belonged to the workers movement, persecuted by Mussolini's Blackshirts. The symbols change but the substance remains: fear is a great instrument for collective manipulation, and it is what should most concern us—because tomorrow those reputed to be "different" could be us.

CHAPTER 13

A NEW ECONOMIC MODEL

WEALTH GONE UP IN SMOKE

At the root of the credit crisis one finds a major economic illusion: the trading of risk—deriving from the activity of either banks or financial institutions—as if risk represented a type of asset or merchandise and its buying and selling could generate wealth and economic growth. Among the fictitious assets produced by the trading of risk are stocks and bonds structured using subprime mortgages and packaged together, as well as those created using commodities indices and credit default swaps. These fake financial products have been exchanged in the markets for years. Derivatives calculated their value and price, often using complex formulas taken from quantum physics or chaos theory.

As opposed to traditional stocks or bonds, the purpose of which are to secure credit for the growth of the private or public sector, these imaginary assets ended up being used by those who produced and sold them to inflate profits and to enable greater credit leverage. For years, people believed that this trade, which developed electronically, created wealth. Today we know that it produced only the ephemeral illusion of wealth.

The credit crunch and recession destroyed all the wealth accumulated over the last twenty years. This erosion took place both in financial and monetary terms. As the values of shares diminish, available credit contracts until it disappears. Here are some indicative figures: through March 2009, banks had lost $2 trillion, the stock market $30 trillion, the real estate sector $4 trillion, and industrial production had decreased by about $3 trillion.

What's burning is not only this illusory, electronically created wealth but, more importantly, real wealth. When the shares of an international bank like Citigroup drop from seventy dollars to two dollars a share, it means that most of the money that savers had invested has disappeared. Share prices not only function as the barometer of a company's management, they also mark its worth. The same holds true for all listed companies. This explains why governments persist in trying to save the financial sector. Any antirecession maneuver will fail if finance continues to crumble. The common response of Western governments to this economic cataclysm has been the transfer of bad risk accumulated by the private sector to the balance sheet of the state, a strategy that does not work for obvious reasons.

THE GREAT BAILOUT

Instead of eliminating risk, excising it like a cancer from the global economy, the state is merely shifting it from one sector to another—from the private to the public—making the situation worse. It's clear that this policy hides a deep-rooted desire to maintain the status quo, thereby saving an economy at all costs and the system upon which it rests, in which the creation and the trading of risk cannot be altered. The economic conditions that transformed risk into an asset have all disappeared: the aggressive merchandising of credit at rock-bottom prices, which stemmed from the deflationary policy that the Fed had pursued since the fall of the Berlin Wall, and the growth of structured financial products that transformed risk into a marketable asset. Indeed this was a distortion, an anomaly that should have been corrected over a decade ago. Even better, it should never have taken place.

Let us not forget that finance is a zero-sum game, which, as opposed to the real economy, does not create wealth but merely distributes it. Financial markets also offer, via stock market quotations, a snapshot of the performance of companies and of the productive sectors. It would have been enough to keep this concept in mind to understand that the multiplication of risk had nothing to do with economic growth but represented a danger to all.

When credit dried up, balance sheet risk could not be traded any longer so banks' and financial companies' exposure rose enormously, to the point that in many cases it has become unmanageable. The so-called "toxic assets" that the state keeps buying are high-risk packages that represent an ever-increasing loss for those who hold them. Financial stimulus packages that use taxpayers' money and the printing machines of the central banks should be regarded for what they are: financial hemorrhaging that does not heal the wound but merely empties the public coffers and mortgages the wealth of our children. In March 2009, the share prices of companies and banks "saved" by governments were all below the levels at which the state had purchased them. Will they ever get back to the heights of the last few years? Economists seem very skeptical.

A SYSTEM THAT DOES NOT WORK

The world is still far from recognizing the absurdity of a system based upon anachronistic economic principles, such as the trading of risk or the belief that Western workers benefit from buying goods produced by Chinese workers. Equally absurd is the conviction that the economy benefits from a growing Western demand entirely financed by borrowing money originating from the high saving ratio of Chinese workers, who since 2001 have sustained the growth of America's public-sector debt. Who can deny that Americans and other Westerners consumed foreign goods and services for more than a decade, increasing their indebtedness from abroad and jeopardizing in the long run their own work, their income, and their ability to repay the debt? The relation between debt and income, debt and wealth, has become unmanageable, both for the banks and for the population as a whole. How do we bring it back to acceptable levels? Certainly not by pumping money into the balance sheets of banks and finance companies.

The "dismal science" is not an exact science, but it is at least based upon the rationality of individuals. At this time we should ask ourselves not only if it is right but also if it is reasonable to save all the banks and anyone who might be losing their home. Is it economically beneficial to recapitalize companies that have lost the capacity to supply to society that service for which they were created: credit? For years, banks like Citigroup and the British HBOS, as well as companies such as AIG, the largest American insurer, have behaved like hedge funds or stockbrokerages and not like lenders, to the extent that they have forgotten how to perform their own profession.

We should ask ourselves if it makes sense in economic terms to extend mortgage payments on houses when their values are less than the mortgage principal outstanding, when the resident owners would save money by renting an identical property down the block at a cost far well below their current mortgage payments. So many of these residences have been acquired without capital, with 100 percent mortgages; abandoning them means losing only the paid installments and nothing more. We should consider this "loss" as rent paid rather than as a social defeat.

But before arriving at a conclusion that might appear excessively radical and insensitive to the social problems facing those who are losing the roofs over their heads, let us dust off our economic knowledge and reread what Adam Smith wrote about real estate. The father of liberal doctrine clearly stated that real estate cannot be a source of wealth. Even when properties are rented out, the monetary gain springs from another activity, a productive one. As opposed to the neoliberal creed, Adam Smith did not consider consumption as a primary source of wealth. Were he alive today, he would judge China to be a far wealthier nation than America because China produces while America consumes. This leads us to another malfunction in the current economic model: the engine of Western economic growth is no longer production but consumption.

But there is another myth to debunk: the illusion that real estate assets generate wealth over time, that the mere fact that they exist gives them value. This is also a modern fantasy. Statistics show that until just after World War II it was more economical to rent than to buy a house. The increase in rents and property values resulted from an economy that suffered first because of the inflation generated by two oil crises before it then fell victim to the financial bubble. If economic history is not just an opinion, then it stands to reason that for the next few decades house values will not return to the levels of 2006 and we will be fortunate if they settle, adjusted for inflation, at around those of the early 1970s.

In this vision, making payments on mortgages exceeding the value of the underlying property is a folly because by doing so one essentially finances a negative investment. But no one wants to believe this truth, just as no one wanted to believe that it was crazy to trade risk. Thus at the beginning of 2009, US Secretary of the Treasury Timothy Geithner declared to Congress that the rescue of banks and the new president's financial stimulus package sought to sustain housing prices, to put them back on track to resume their unrelenting growth. Even the law of supply and demand tells us that this is an illusion. In the US over the last years, too many houses have been built. From Las Vegas to New York, from Denver to Miami, real estate speculation has seen to it that supply far outpaces demand, and, as a result, prices fall.

One can make an analogous analysis of the policy of saving the banks. No one seems ready for nationalization, therefore various alternative strategies are employed. These include the purchase of preferential shares and their conversion, in some cases, into standard shares at above-market prices, as happened with Citigroup in March 2009. This was a way of injecting additional funds into the banks' negative balance sheets without becoming a majority shareholder. These are magic tricks, not dissimilar from those we have seen before and which brought us to this crisis. Behind this dissimulation is a depressing reality: governments only know one economic doctrine, and they apply it without fully appreciating the consequences. As Nobel Prize–winning economist Paul Krugman wrote, the politicians do not want to admit that the system doesn't work and must be radically changed.

The indiscriminate support of all the banks without a reasoned policy of nationalization only serves to destroy wealth. The proof is that no rescued American bank, and surely no rescued European one, is in a position today to pay dividends to the preferred shareholders as Obama had hoped. On the contrary, they all find themselves in economic difficulty and are asking for more money. The desire to maintain, at any cost, a damaged and anachronistic system will only bring ruination. Countries such as Italy, hit by recession but as yet far from the banking collapse, should understand this lesson. To follow in the footsteps of the Americans and the British would be disastrous.

So how to break this downward spiral? First of all, it is necessary to accept that we have been in a recessive phase already for several months and that, because this is a systemic and not a situational crisis, the recession will last much longer than the others. From the end of the Second World War until now, the duration of economic crises in fact has decreased, which has led many to believe that this one will be short too. But they are wrong. The current recession is already in its fourteenth month, the fourth since 1945 to exceed twelve months. Only the crisis of the oil aftershock of 1973–74 and the recession of 1981 reached sixteen months. The Great Depression, the longest in modern history, lasted forty-three months—almost four years. Many economists think that we will be living with this recession for all of 2009 and part of 2010.

HOW DO WE GET OUT OF THE CRISIS?

The policies carried out today, however, are short-term policies because politicians' horizons are short. They are merely Band-Aids slapped on severed arteries. If we ask to think in terms of years, not months, then everything changes. Pumping money into banking monoliths like Citigroup, HBOS, and some of the larger European banks makes no sense because the economy will continue to contract and these banks will not manage to survive for the simple reason that what kept them standing, and in fact caused them to grow, were financial games not traditional banking activity.

We should use instead this long recessive period to restructure the financial system, pruning all the deadwood accumulated over the last two decades and preparing for regrowth. We should nationalize the banking sector and save only that part which serves to keep the economy afloat. Once the storm has passed, what will prevent their privatization? This is what many economists, including Krugman, are suggesting; but the word nationalization still seems to be synonymous with socialism. Those who have followed this path, such as the UK, have done so only because there was no alternative, and soon even the US will find itself in a similar situation. In the meantime, the government will have burned almost $3 trillion dollars of taxpayers' money. The nationalization of the banks is inevitable but should be carried out wisely. Our money could be used to save the commercial banking sector, in which our savings are stored, and not investment banking folly.

Finance should be reformed with clear policies and now, not in some hypothetical future. If derivatives led to the creation of toxic assets then why not outlaw them? Why should taxpayers be required to rescue insurance companies that acted like hedge funds, which created and sold credit default swaps—in reality, little different than bets at the green-felt tables in a casino—without having the capital to back them up? The state should abolish these products and separate out the insurance operations from these companies letting the gambling side go bust. The losses will most affect those who were most exposed to risk—the banks and the financiers of chance, the deadwood of which we would like to rid ourselves. One look at AIG well illustrates this concept. A large part of the $180 billion it received has ended up in the vaults of the banks that held the credit default swaps that AIG could not honor. Neither the insurance company nor the American government wanted to publicize the names of the beneficiaries, but Wall Street knew well that they were ex-investment banks such as Goldman Sachs and Merrill Lynch. If high finance was happy to gamble, let them pay the consequences of this folly instead of soaking up the money needed to restart the economy.

These strategies would be enough to clean up many balance sheets, those of banks and serious companies. But this requires the direct intervention of the state, and no one seems to be disposed to do so. In fact, what is missing is a strong state, which is not scared of dictating the new rules of the game and of the ghosts of socialism. What we need is a state that knows how to extract—from liberal theory, Marxist theory, and classical Keynesian capitalism—those instruments and ideas that are necessary to drag us out of this financial quagmire.

Why not also borrow some of the principles of Islamic finance: that money should always be invested in or connected to the real economy? Speculation based on indices, for example, in which packages of securities are bought and sold without any regard for the performance of the underlying companies, is destroying real wealth. Companies quoted on the NASDAQ or on Wall Street are sucked into the whirlpool of sectorial decline even when they show good profits, only because they are traded via indices. The same is happening in all the markets. This is another activity to be abolished.

But in order to accomplish this, one needs a state that protects its own citizens, not the institutions that have brought about their misery: a state that takes finance in hand, not just via nationalization but also by temporarily getting involved in its operation. If the rescued banks don't lend more money, if the injections of liquidity that are eroding the finances of the state end up only on the banks' balance sheets, then the state should strengthen cooperative banks and local banks; it should deposit in their vaults the money that has been lost up to now in the salvaging of the big banks. These are credit institutions that are founded on solid codes of ethics and that have maintained the social role of banks to gather and distribute wealth, thereby promoting economic growth. The network of branches of these banks is like a network of capillaries covering a large part of the nation. If this is not enough, then the state should create a parallel banking network using post office counters, transforming these into bank branches. In fact, this task is similar to what the Federal Reserve is doing de facto with commercial paper—industrial sector securities—which it now discounts directly.

If this rationalization of the banking sector further damages the already devastated pension funds, then the state should get involved and guarantee those who have been robbed, not rewarding instead those who have wasted bank deposits. The remaining pensions should be transferred into state funds, managed by the nationalized companies.

THE REAL ECONOMY

So we come to the sector of the real economy. Here the greatest enemy is unemployment. During the Great Depression, around 20 million people lost their jobs in the US alone. It is possible that unemployment figures today will reach close to 20 percent almost everywhere, therefore it is imperative to have an action plan against this phenomenon. Forget about unemployment compensation—better to use the money to finance the restructuring of the labor force. Why pay someone to do nothing? Let's pay the unemployed, but also the recent graduates, who do not even make it to the unemployment rolls and aren't entitled to this compensation, to learn the skills of tomorrow. The state should produce a long-term plan for the industrial conversion to clean energy and heavy investment in infrastructure. It should relaunch and restructure the productive sector. The automobile industry, for example, is stuck in the Stone Age, when oil cost less than Coca-Cola. Even the service and agricultural sectors are in need of reform. The food crisis of 2008 made us understand how much our food depends on energy costs.

All of these reforms require great sacrifice, and it will be the people who will have to make them. But how can governments hope to gain the support of the taxpayer when the latter is still being lied to? Statistics in the US demonstrate that about 70 percent of saved mortgages fall back into arrears in a few months. Too many people live in houses that they could not—and cannot—afford, and the state cannot change this reality. Moreover, too many people live in housing that will continue to decline in value for a long time. America and the world must wake up to this truth.

If anyone thinks that this type of intervention will demand too much money, then it should be sufficient to consider two points: first, there is plenty of money around because all the central banks are printing it; second, and even more importantly, the cost of rescuing the banks is potentially immense. The facts bear this out. In the six months following the fall of Lehman Brothers, the world lost 5 percent of the global GDP, almost $3 trillion. During the same period, $2 trillion was inserted into banks via the rescue plans, money that has been swallowed by the banks' negative balance sheets. Now economic growth has declined to levels not seen since before the recession of the early 1980s. The cost of rescuing the American banks in the last quarter of 2008 was equivalent to 5 percent of the US's GDP, and the British banks equivalent to 3 percent of the UK's GDP. These figures are dramatically higher than those of the past. Norway's 1990–93 crisis cost it 8 percent of its GDP, Sweden's 1991–96 crisis cost it 6.5 percent of its GDP, and Japan's crisis of 1997–2003 cost it 8 percent of its GDP. At this rate, America will have spent, in 2009 alone, more than 10 percent of its GDP just to support the financial sector, without this vast expense even minimally impacting the real economy.

America is a country where labor mobility has always been high. Someone who loses a job in Wisconsin and who might have a good job prospect in Texas jumps in her car and goes. President Roosevelt's New Deal worked thanks to this type of migration. But if people are tied to mortgages in an illiquid market, how will they be able to move? President Obama's plan to delay mortgage payments in high-risk cases, therefore, runs the risk of reducing labor mobility at the very moment in which it is crucial for the success of the public works program. Since the fall of the Berlin Wall, even Europe has seen an increase in labor mobility. Policies that limit or reduce this will be counterproductive.

There is a way out of this vise, which since the beginning of the millennium has been strangling us, and it is different from the road we have taken so far. It is time that someone has the courage to lead the way.

BIBLIOGRAPHIC NOTES

DUBAI: THE RISE OF ISLAMIC FINANCE

Ayub, Muhammad. *Understanding Islamic Finance*. New York: Wiley, 2008.

Cattori, Silvia. "The Incredible Story of Youssef Nada." Silvia Cattori, http://www.silviacattori.net/article461.html.

Davidson, Christopher. *The Vulnerability of Success*. New York: Columbia University Press, 2008.

"Dubai, Inc.," *60 Minutes*, DVD. New York: CBS, 2007.

El-Gamal, Mahmoud A. *Islamic Finance: Law, Economics, and Practice*. Cambridge, MA: Cambridge University Press, 2008.

Hosenball, Mark. "Terror's Cash Flow: Is Al Taqwa, A Shadowy Financial Network, A Secret Money Machine For Osama Bin Laden?" *Newsweek*. March 25, 2002.

Iqbal, Zamir, and Abbas Mirakhor. *An Introduction to Islamic Finance: Theory and Practice*. New York: Wiley, 2008.

Komisar, Lucy. "Shareholders in the Bank of Terror?" Salon. March 25, 2002. http://dir.salon.com/story/tech/feature/2002/03/15/al_taqua/index.html.

Ridgeway, James. *The 5 Unanswered Questions About 9/11: What the 9/11 Commission Failed to Tell Us*. New York: Seven Stories Press, 2005.

Sisti, Leo. *Caccia a Bin Laden*. Milan: Baldini & Castoldi, 2004.

"The 9/11 Investigations." Public Affairs Reports. New York, 2004.

"The 9/11 Commission Report." National Commission on Terrorist Attacks upon the United States. http://www.9-11commission.gov/report/911Report.pdf

THE WAR ON TERROR: AMERICA'S SUICIDAL MISSION
(From a lecture at Rosemont College in Philadelphia, October 2003.)

Baer, Robert. *See No Evil*. Santa Barbara: Crown, 2002.

Landau, Saul. *The Pre-Emptive Empire*. London: Pluto Press, 2003.

Meacher, Michael. "This War on Terrorism is Bogus." *The Guardian*. September 6, 2003. http://www.guardian.co.uk/politics/2003/sep/06/September11.iraq

"Rebuilding America's Defenses: Strategy, Forces and Resources for a New Century," Project for the New American Century. http://www.newamericancentury.org/RebuildingAmericasDefenses.pdf

Scowen, Peter. *Rogue Nation*. Toronto: M&S, 2002.

Suskind, Ron. *I segreti della Casa Bianca*. Milan: Il Saggiatore, 2004.

Unger, Craig. *House of Bush, House of Saud*. New York: Scribner, 2003.

THE REVERSAL OF THE CRUSADES
(From an essay written for *SAIS Review*, Spring/Fall 2003.)

Armstrong, Karen. *Holy War: The Crusades and Their Impact on Today's World*. New York: Anchor Books, 2001.

Atiya, Aziz. *Crusade, Commerce and Culture*. Bloomington: Indiana University Press, 1962.

Barber, Michael. *The Two Cities*. London: Routledge, 1992.

Brown, Peter. *The Rise of Western Christendom*. Oxford: Blackwell, 2003. Trad. it. *La formazione dell'Europa cristiana: universalismo e diversita, 200–1000 d.C.* Roma-Bari: *Editori Laterza*, 1995.

Fletcher, Richard. *The Cross and the Crescent*. London: Penguin Books, 2003. Trad. it. *Cristianesimo e islam a confronto: mille anni di storia fra Maometto e l'eta moderna*. Milan: Corbaccio, 2003.

Jacquard, Roland. *Au nom d'Oussama Ben Laden . . . : dossier secret sur le terroriste le plus recherché du monde*. Paris: Picollec, 2001.

Kruegar, Hilmar C. "Economic Aspects of Expanding Europe." in *Twelfth-Century Europe and the Foundations of Modern Society*, edited by Marshall Clagett, Gaines Post, and Robert Reynolds. Madison, WI: University of Wisconsin Press, 1961.

Lewis, Bernard. *The Muslim Discovery of Europe*. New York: W. W. Norton & Company, 2001.

Lopez, Roberto S. *The Commercial Revolution of the Middle Ages, 950–1350.* Englewood Cliffs, NJ: Prentice-Hall, 1971. Trad. it. *La rivoluzione commerciale del Medioevo,* Torino: Einaudi, 1975.

Maalouf, Amin. *The Crusades Through Arab Eyes.* New York: Schocken Books, 1984.

Napoleoni, Loretta. *Terror Inc.* New York: Seven Stories Press, 2005. Trad. it. *Terrorismo S.p.A.* Milan: Tropea, 2005.

Paz, Reuven. "Middle East Islamism in the European Arena," *Middle East Review of International Affairs* 3 (September 2002): 74.

Pinzuti, Marzia. "Il Sogno del Mercato Comune Arabo," *Limes* (2003): 117–125.

Pirenne, Henri. *Le città del Medioevo.* Roma-Bari: Laterza, 1973.

Popescu, Maria Magdelena and Suha Mustafa. "The Gulf Monetary Unification: Opportunities and Challenges," *Arab Bank Review 3* (April 2001).

Pounds, Norman J. *An Economic History of Medieval Europe.* London: Longman,1974.

Rashid, Ahmed. *Jihad: The Rise of Militant Islam in Central Asia.* New Haven, CT: Yale University Press, 2002. Trad. it. *Nel cuore dell'Islam: geopolitica e movimenti estremisti in Asia centrale.* Milan: Feltrinelli, 2002.

Reston, James. *Warriors of God.* New York: Anchor Books, 2002.

Runciman, Steven, *A History of the Crusades.* Vol. 1. London: Folio, 1994. Trad. it. *Storia delle Crociate.* Torino: Einaudi, 2005.

Sampson, Anthony. *The Seven Sisters, The Great Oil Companies and the World They Made.* London: Hodder and Stoughton, 1975. Trad. it. *Le sette sorelle: le grandi compagnie petrolifere e il mondo che hanno creato.* Milan: Mondadori, 1976.

Wasserman, James, *The Templars and the Assassins: The Militia of Heaven,* Rochester, VT: Inner Traditions International, 2001.

International Monetary Fund's Statistics, http://ifs.apdi.net/imf/logon/aspx

"President Bush's Religious Rhetoric." PBS. March 21, 2003, http://www.pbs.org/wnet/religionandethics/week623/news.html (March 23, 2003).

Remarks by Attorney General Ashcroft, September 16, 2001, www.whitehouse.gov/news/releases2001/0920010916.html (March 24, 2003).

BLEEDING AMERICA BANKRUPT: BIN LADEN FULFILLS HIS DREAM
(From a series of lectures in Copenhagen at the Military School in Monterey, CA, and at the Police Academy in Barcelona.)

Abuza, Zachary. *Militant Islam in Southeast Asia: Crucible of Terror.* London: Lynne Rienner, 2003.

Chandler, Michael, and Rohan Gunaratna. *Countering Terrorism.* London: Reaktion Books, 2007.

"Losses inflicted on Saudi investors following September 11th attacks in the US." *Arabic News,* November 21, 2001. http://www.arabicnews.com/ansub/Daily/Day/011121/2001112104.html

Randal, Jonathan. *Osama: The Making of a Terrorist.* New York: Knopf, 2004.

Steavenson, Wendell. "Inside the Mind of a Terrorist." *The Sunday Times.* September 2004.

Stiglitz, Joseph. "It's not the economy, stupid." *Financial Times.* September 28, 2008.

THE USA PATRIOT ACT: A SLEF-INFLICTED WOUND
(From the report of the Working Group on Combating the Financing of Terrorism, chaired by the author, at the Club de Madrid, 2005.)

Baker, Raymond W. *Capitalism's Achilles Heel: Dirty Money and How to Renew the Free-Market System.* New York: Wiley, 2005.

Buchanan, Pat. *Where the Right Went Wrong: How Neoconservatives Subverted the Reagan Revolution and Hijacked the Bush Presidency.* New York: Thomas Dunne Books, 2004.

Lilley, Peter. *Dirty Dealing.* Sterling, VA: Kogan Page, 2003.

Organisation for Economic Co-operation and Development. "Economic consequences of terrorism," http://www.oecd.org/dataoecd/11/60/1935314.pdf

"US Patriot Act." Financial Crimes Enforcement Network. http://www.fincen.gov/statures_regs/patriot/index.html

OIL AS A RETALIATORY WEAPON
(From articles published in *D di Repubblica, Internazionale, La Stampa, Mondo e Missione.*)

Deffeys, Kenneth S. *Hubbert's Peak: The Impending World Oil Reserves.* Princeton, NJ: Princeton University Press, 2003.

Mueller, John. *Overblown: How Politicians and the Terrorism Industry Inflate National Security Threats and Why We Believe Them.* New York: Free Press, 2006.

Simmons, Matt. "New Study Raises Doubts about Saudi Oil Reserves." The Institute for the Analysis of Global Security. March 31, 2004.

SCENES FROM A GLOBAL HOUSE OF CARDS
(From articles published in *D di Repubblica, Internazionale, Chicago Tribune.*)

Napoleoni, Loretta. *Rogue Economics: Capitalism's New Reality.* New York: Seven Stories Press, 2008.

Napoleoni Loretta. *Terror Incorporated: Tracing the Dollars Behind the Terror Networks.* New York: Seven Stories Press, 2005.

Statistics from Bloomberg.com.

THE POLITICS OF FEAR
(From the speeches at the Festival of Literature in Mantua, September 2008, and at the University of New Mexico, October 2008.)

Napoleoni, Loretta. *I numeri del terrore.* Milan: Il Saggiatore, 2008.

Napoleoni Loetta. *Insurgent Iraq: Al-Zarqawi and the New Generation.* New York: Seven Stories Press, 2005.

INDEX

Afghanistan, xii, xviii
    cost of US troops in, xix
    drug business in, 69
    invasion of, 61
    shell states of, 66
    war, xvii, xix, 2, 39
African National Congress, xiv
agriculture
    energy v., 91
    futures market of, 91
Ahmadinejad, Mahmoud, 90
AIG, 149
Albania, 51–52
Algeria, 34
aliens, 139, 140
American Express Gold, 106
anti-terrorism
    against Bank al-Taqwa, 28
    legislation of, 67
    monetary controls of post 9/11, 12
apartheid, xiv
Ashcroft, John, 34
Asprey, 95–96
assets
    imaginary, 141
    toxic, 143
Atta, Mohamed, 20, 22, 121, 131
AUC. See United Self-Defense Forces
    of Colombia
automobile industry, 151

Baghdad, 110
Bahamas, Islamic finance in, 21–29
Bahamian Central Bank, Bank al-
    Taqwa license revocation by, 25
bailout, xix, 142–43
Baker, Raymond, 48
Bank al-Taqwa, 21
    before 9/11, 25–27

anti-terrorist measures against, 28
history of, 23–24
investigation of, 22–23, 25, 28–29
license revocation of, 25
name change of, 26
shareholders of, 27
Swiss Federal Bank review of, 25
Bank of England, 99
bankruptcy, of US, 81
banks, 150. See also specific types
    British, 152
    competition among, 105–6
    of Dubai, 12–13
    European, 148
    GDP v., 151–52
    international, 86–87
    Iranian, 52
    Islamic, 15, 16, 17, 19, 29, 36
    Islamization of, 18
    loans, 105–6
    losses, 142
    Malaysian, 17–19
    nationalization v., 146–47, 148
    offshore, 21, 75
    Patriot Act v., 76
    saving, 146, 151–52
    sharia compliance of, 16, 18, 19
    superrich of, 107
    US, 152
    Western, 19
    Western v. Islamic, 51
Basque Euskadi Ta Askatsuna (ETA), xv
Basra, 88
beheadings, 57–58
    post 9/11, 59
Berlin Wall, xvi, xviii, 112, 113, 138
Bert the Turtle, 113
bin Laden, Osama, xii, 6, 55, 60–61,
    114–15, 135

in cold war, role of, 35
Erwa's information about, 37–38
fatwa of Saudi Arabia, 86
foreign policy *v.*, 38
Hussein *v.*, 61
justification of terrorism, 42
neutralization of, 38
propaganda of, 37, 85
Saudi Arabia and, 35
speeches of, 41
in Sudan, 36
warrant for, 36, 37
Washington's relationship with, 35
bin Mohamad, Mahathir, 17–18
bin Salih al-Jarbou, Adb al-Aziz, 55
black market
American economy *v.*, 74
growth of, 77–78
Black Tuesday, 24
Blair, Tony, 7
accusations against, 32
architectural heritage of, 97
blood, 58
Bohemund, Count, 45
"The Bomb in the Backyard," 114–15
Bonfire of Vanities (Wolfe), 92
bonuses, multimillion-dollar, 123
Brown, Gordon, 98, 137
Buchanan, Pat, 80, 81
budget
of Pentagon, annual, 80
surplus, 1
The Bulgari Collection (Weldon), 96
Bush, George W., xiv, 1, 7, 22, 26, 79
9/11 rhetoric of, 40, 42, 69
accusations against, 32
Buchanan on foreign policy of, 80
criticism of Clinton, xviii
dollar value decline *v.*, 89–90
of Federal Reserve, pressuring by, 4
ignorance of, 59
interest rate slashing of, 106
legacy of, 71
post 9/11 speech, 139
secrecy *v.* cooperation of, 28–29
ulterior motives of, 31–32
Bush, Jeb, 32
Bush Administration. *See* Bush,
George W.

caliphate, 59, 60
capital flight, illegal, 48, 65
capitalism, 7, 17, 136
contemporary, 109
credit crunch *v.*, 109–10
destroying icons of, 57–58
Islamic finance and western, 14–18
spread of, 65
symbolic targets of, 70
CBI. *See* Central Bank of Iran
Central Bank of Iran (CBI), 52
Central Intelligence Agency (CIA),
xvi, 33
bankrolling of anti-Soviet jihad, 35
Chávez, Hugo, 90
Cheney, Dick, 32
children, propaganda for, 113
China, xiii, 6, 145
US dependence on, xiii
Christendom, 53
Christianity, 45, 53–54
"Chub," 79
CIA. *See* Central Intelligence Agency
Citigroup, 142, 144, 146, 147
citizens
protection of, 150
state *v.*, 4
Clarke, Nicky, 96
"clash of civilizations," 18, 118, 138
classes, rise of new commercial,
49–52
Clinton, Bill, xviii
CNN, 117
cold war, xvi, xviii, 34–35, 65
anatomy of, 110–15
bin Laden's role in, 35
Colombian drug cartels, Patriot Act *v.*,
78
colonization
decolonization, 46
Islamic, 36–37
commodity market, 87
Communism, 39
Communist Bloc, 112
comparative advantage, 136
Congo, 125
Congress, power of US, 71
consumerism, 110
cooperation, secrecy *v.*, 28–29
Cortesi, Filippo, 84, 87

credit
    cards, 106
    crisis, root of, 141
    institutions, 150
    institutions, Islamic, 17–18
    lack of, 143
    selling, 105
credit crunch, xii, xix, 3, 5, 7, 109, 135
    capitalism v., 109–10
    destruction of, 142
    Dubai and, 11–12
    effect on Britain, 99
    ignorance at root of, 59–60
    private school enrollment v., 94
    seeds of, 77
    terrorism v., 14
    war on terror v., 34
crusades
    economic decay v., 43–46, 56
    First, 42–43, 45, 46, 50, 54
    Fourth, 50
    jihad v., 41–43, 49
    mobilizing power of, 54
    role reversal of, 58–59
    social transformation offered by, 53
Cuban missile crisis, 112
currency
    US v. other, 76–77
    world's reserve, 74

death
    penalty, terrorism v., xv
    toll in Iraq, 116
    toll of war on terror, 67
debt, xii
    ballooning, 74
    GNP v., 76–77
    income v., 144
    Patriot Act v., 74–75
    public, 144
    securitization of, 5
    treasury bonds and, 4
    US, xix, 1, 4, 39, 80, 108
decolonization, 46
deflation, 3, 5, 105, 143
democracy, xii, xviii–xix, 46–47
    exporting principles of, 67, 71
deregulation, 16–17, 65, 71
Dhabi, Abu, 11
DIGOS. See Division for General

Investigations and Special Operations
diversity, fear of, 138–40
Division for General Investigations
    and Special Operations
    (DIGOS), 24–25
dollar(s)
    beneficiaries of weak, 88–90
    declining demand of, 76–77
    devaluation effect on Europe,
      89–90
    euro v., 63, 99
    exodus from, 76–77
    gold-exchange standard of, 81
    money laundering US, 73–75
    post 9/11 value of, 62, 76–77
    transactions, Patriot Act monitor-
      ing of, 75–76, 78, 99–100
    value, Bush v. declining, 89–90
    value, Patriot Act v., 62
    yuan v., 89
drugs, xii, 69
Dubai
    9/11 and, 12–14, 132
    banks of, 12–13
    credit crunch and, 11–12
    Islamic finance hub in, 11–21
    Las Vegas v., 121, 129–33
    marketing strategy of, 125
    real estate in, 122, 123, 124, 126
    as tax haven, 122, 124
    tourism in, 122
    unemployment in, 127

economic crisis
    of 1930s, 135–37
    getting out of, 147–50
economic domination, Islamic, 44
economic evolution, 49
economy
    America's responsibility to world,
      138
    bailout and, 142–43
    black, 73
    black market v. American, 74
    crusades v. decay of, 43–46, 56
    cyclical nature of, 136
    faulty system of, 144–47
    gasoline prices v., 64
    imbalance of Muslim, 47

interconnectedness of, 116–17
Iraq's insurgency, 68
Islamic, 15
of Las Vegas, 122
MBS v., 108
out-of-control, 87, 131
Patriot Act damage to European, 77
Patriot Act v. US, 76–77
real, 149–52
recession of, 5–7, 71, 81, 94, 136,
    142, 147
of terror, 65–71, 73–75
terrorism v., xiii, xvi, 3, 131
of United Arab Emirates, 13
of US, 6
Vietnam consequences on, 80–81
war on terror's consequences for,
    60–63, 79–81
Egypt, 34, 84
employment, 63–64. *See also* unem-
    ployment
energy
    agriculture v., 91
    clean, 151
    costs, 83
    crisis, 84, 91
England
    banks of, 152
    credit crunch effect on, 99
    private schools of, 93–94
    taxation laws of, 97–99
entertainment industry, 128
Erwa, Elfatih, General, 37–38
ethics, 150
    finance v., 16–17
EU. *See* European Union
euro, 90
    dollar v., 63, 99
    money laundering and, 77–78
Europe
    commercial revolution of
        Western, 50
    dollar devaluation's effect on,
        89–90
    imports v. exports of, 44
    as money laundromat for world,
        75–76
    Patriot Act v. economy of, 77
    wars on Western, 44–45
European Central Bank, 90

European Union (EU)
    English tax laws v., 98
    money regulations, lack of, 79
executions, public, 59
Executive Order 13224, 26
export(s), 137
    democracy as, 67, 71
    European v. Muslim, 44
    US v. Chinese, 89

fatwa, 16, 19, 86
FBI. *See* Federal Bureau of Investiga-
    tion
fear, 7, 138
    danger of, 85–87
    of diversity, 138–40
    futures market v., 87–88
    of nuclear war, 112–14
    politicians strategy of, 111–12
    politics of, 119
    propaganda of, 111–13
    Roosevelt on, 135
    root of, 117–18
    of terrorism, 2–3, 87–88, 114,
        115–19, 135
Federal Bureau of Investigation (FBI),
    33
    discovery of al-Qaeda's reconnais-
        sance videos, 61
Federal Civil Defense Administration,
    113
Federal Reserve, 74, 150
    Bush administration pressuring
        of, 4
    interest rate cuts of, 77
Fergana Valley, 49
feudal system, after fall of Roman Em-
    pire, 43–44
films, US propaganda, 113
finance
    ethics v., 16–17
    globalized, 135
    of al-Qaeda, 65
    terrorist, 23, 27–28, 67, 68–69,
        77–78
    of war on terror, Chinese, 89
finance, Islamic, 6, 20, 124
    in Bahamas, 21–29
    capital increase in, 18–19
    Dubai as hub of, 11–21

growth of, 19
post 9/11 boom in, 18–20
principles of, 149
religion v., 15–16
western capitalism and, 14–18
finance, western, 20
code of ethics in, 16–17
financial industry, gambling v., 123
financial system, restructuring, 148
First Crusade, 42–43, 45, 46, 50, 54
food
crisis, 90–92, 151
prices, surge in, 90–92
foreclosures, in Las Vegas, 126
foreign exchange earnings, 47–48
foreign investment, 48
foreign policy
bin Laden v., 38
Buchanan on Bush's, 80
Washington's aggressive, 32–33, 39, 62
Foreign Policy, 114–15
Fourth Crusade, 50
French Revolution, 59
fundamentalism, Islamic, 54–55
role of, 85
futures market
fear v., 87–88
food and agriculture sectors of, 91
rollover in, 91–92
speculative use of, 92
supply and demand v. rising prices of, 87

G-20. *See* Group of Twenty
al-Gaddafi, Muammar, 37
gambling, 148
decline in, 125
financial industry v., 123
legal, 121–22
mathematics of, 129
in US, 122–23
gangs, 139
Garden House, 93–94
Garon, Jesse, 128–29
gasoline, prices of, 64. *See also* oil
GDP. *See* gross domestic product
Geithner, Timothy, 146
Gekko, Gordon, 124
Ghamr, Mit, 15

globalization, 3, 5, 35, 39, 67, 100, 125, 128
finance and, 135
homogenization of, 139
Islamic colonization as side-effect of, 36–37
superrich and, 12, 93–94, 95, 97
thieves v. simpletons of, 110
gold
exchange standard, end of, 81
smuggling of Congolese, 124–25
Goldman Sachs, xi, 149
government. *See also* Bush, George W.
bailout of, 142–43
wealth contraction v., 136
government bonds, 75
Great Depression, 137, 140, 147, 150–51
Green, Michael, 127
Greenspan, Alan, 3, 5, 64
response to Patriot Act, 74–75
Grice, Jesse, 127–29
gross criminal product, 65
gross domestic product (GDP), 1
banks v., 151–52
debt percentage of, 80
international, 65
post 9/11, 63
Group of Twenty (G-20), 99
Guardian, 139
Gulf War, 35, 86, 88

hajj, 15
halal, 58
Halliday, John, 97
haram, 14, 16, 58
hedge funds, 88
Helsinki Committee for Human Rights, 52
heroin, xii
hijackers, 9/11, 34, 62
in Las Vegas, 121, 130–31, 132
Himmat, Ali Ghaleb, 24–25, 28
Hitler, Adolf, 118
Holocaust, 118
Hoover, Herbert, 137
hostages, 58
House of Saud, 35–36, 59
hundred-dollar bill, 73
hunger, world, 90–92

Huntington, Samuel, 18, 40, 118
Hussein, Saddam, 32, 46, 66, 131
    bin Laden *v.*, 61
    funding by, 67
    WMD *v.*, 68, 111, 136

IDB. *See* Turkish Islamic Develop-
    ment Bank
ignorance, 118
Il Corriere della Sera, 25
illegal capital flight, 48, 65
IMF. *See* International Monetary Fund
import(s)
    European *v.* Muslim, 44
    oil, 68
income
    debt *v.*, 144
    for hajj, percentage of, 15
    post 9/11 decline in annual, 64
industrial production, losses in, 142
Industrial Revolution, 110
inflation, 145–46
interest only loans, 107
interest rates
    Bush administration slashing of,
        106
    cuts, 107
    Federal Reserve cuts of, 77
    low, 4–5, 75, 105, 123
    Qur'an's prohibition of, 14–15, 16
    real estate *v.*, 106–7
International Fertilizer Development
    Center (IFDC), 51–52
International Monetary Fund (IMF),
    17–18, 49
Internet, propaganda, 113, 120
Inter-Services Intelligence (ISI), xii,
    68
investment, foreign, 48
investors, 124
    Muslim, 76
    post 9/11, 18, 62–63
IRA. *See* Irish Republican Army
Iranian Revolution, 86
Iraq, xviii, 32
    cost of US troops in, xix
    death toll in, 116
    exit strategy for, xi
    insurgency economy of, 68
    invasion of, 111, 116

    justification of war in, 114
    preemptive strike against, 84
    shell states of, 66
    war, xi, xix, 2, 39, 84, 85, 114, 116
"The Iraq Effect," 116
Iraqi insurgency, funding of, 67–68
Irish potato famine, 90–91
Irish Republican Army (IRA), xv, 65
ISI. *See* Inter-Services Intelligence
Islam, 15. *See also* finance, Islamic;
    jihad; mujahideen; Muslim oli-
    garchy
    fundamentalist, 54–55
    rhetoric of, 54–55
    ummah of, 15–16
    unification of, 55
Islamic Center, 24
Islamic colonization, 36–37
Islamic Cultural Institute, 24
isolationism, 56
Italian Maritime Republics of Amalfi,
    50
Italy, 147
    money laundering in, 78–79

jihad, 6, 51, 60, 130
    9/11 and, 69–70
    anti-Soviet, xvi–xvii, 35, 54, 57
    Christian Crusades *v.*, 41–43, 49
    modern, 46–49, 54–56
    Saladin's, 56
    surge in, 37
    symbols of, 58–60
    websites for training of, 69
Johns, Susan, 88
Johnson, Lyndon, 1–2
Joseph, Ramzi, xv
J.P. Morgan, xi

Karimov, Islam, 49
Karzai, Hamid, xii
Kennedy, John F., 113
Khobar, attack on, 87, 88
Khodorkovsky, Mikhail, 100
kidnappings, 68, 69
Kissinger, Henry, 84
Kraft, 91
Krugman, Paul, 146, 148

labor mobility, 152

Lancet, 116
Las Vegas
    9/11 hijackers in, 121, 130–31, 132
    attractions of, 127–29
    downfall of, 129
    Dubai *v.*, 121, 129–33
    economy of, 122
    foreclosures in, 126
    Grice in, 127–28
    history of, 128
    mortgages of, 123
    population growth of, 122
    real estate of, 122–24, 126
    tourism, 122
laundering. *See* money laundering
laws
    of England, taxation, 97–99
    friendly, 100
    of religion, 16–17, 60
Lehman Brothers, 11, 95, 101, 151–52
Lewis, Jeffrey, 114
Libby, Lewis "Scooter," 32
lifestyle, of superrich, 94–96
loans, 105–6. *See also* mortgages
    interest only, 107
London
    crime in, 97
    as metropolitan icon of west, 93–
      97
    political indifference of, 97
    post 9/11, 97
    real estate market crash of, 101
    Russian superrich settlers in, 98
    suicide bombing, 69, 139
    as tax haven, 97–99
London Eye, 97

madrassas, 36, 51
Madrid massacre, 69
Magnus, George, 86
Malayasia
    banks of, 17–19
    Islamic economic model of, 17–18
    sukuk issued by, 19
Mancuso, Salvatore, 78
Mandela, Nelson, xiv
Mara Salvatrucha gang, 139
market(s), 143. *See also* black market;
    commodity market; futures mar-
    ket; stock market

instability of global, 62–63
    threat of terrorism *v.*, 83–85
Masters, Michael, 92
MBS. *See* mortgage-backed securities
Meacher, Michael, 32, 33
meat, 58
Mecca, 15
media, 2, 117
    apocalyptic messages of, 115
    propaganda in, 120
Merchant International Group, 85
Merrill Lynch, 64, 87–88, 149
Middle Ages, Islamic economic domi-
    nation during, 44
Middle East, 32
Mieli, Francesca, 94
military, expenses, 2, 80–81. *See also*
    wars
Millennium Dome, 97
MIPT-RAND, 115–16
Mohammed, Khalid Sheikh, xiv, xv
money laundering, 125
    euro and, 77–78
    Europe and, 75–76
    in Italy, 78–79
    Patriot Act to curb, 75–76
    regulations, post 9/11 anti-, 75
    US dollars, 73–75
Monroe, James, 138
mortgage-backed securities (MBS),
    106–8
    economic growth *v.*, 108
mortgages, 101, 144, 146, 151, 152
    bank competition *v.*, 105–6
    credit cards as collateral for, 106
    interest only, 107
    of Las Vegas, 123
    one hundred percent, 106, 123,
      145
    subprime, 5, 75, 106–7, 108, 123,
      141
mosques, 51, 52, 54
Mother Jones, 116
Moussaoui, Zacarias, 34
mujahideen, xvi–xvii, 35, 37, 57
al-Muqatila, 37
Muslim Brotherhood, 130
Muslim elite, 47, 48, 54, 60
Muslim oligarchy, 47, 51, 60
    alliance between West and, 47

economic gap between masses
and, 54
mythology, of terrorism, 119

Nabisco, 91
Nada, Youssef, 24
on terror lists, 28
travel ban on, 28–29
in Vaduz, 28–29
Nada Management, 26
Namangani, Juma, 49
Nasreddin, Ahmed Idris, 24, 28
Nasser, Gamal Abdel, 46
nationalism, protectionism *v.*, 136–37
nationalization, 146–47
banks *v.*, 146–47, 148
socialism *v.*, 148
national security, terrorism *v.*, xiv–xv,
31
Nazis, 118, 140
'Ndrangheta, rise to power of, 78–79
Nevada, suicide rate of, 126
New Deal, 152
New Labour, 97
Newton Prep, 94
9/11, 6, 17, 29. *See also* hijackers, 9/11
aftermath of, 22, 83, 98–99, 115
America's response to, 14, 31, 56,
63–64, 79, 105
anti-money-laundering regulations, post, 75
anti-terrorism monetary controls
of post, 12
Bank al-Taqwa before, 25–27
as blueprint for terrorist attack,
69–70
broadcasting of, 117
Bush's rhetoric about, 40, 42, 69
Bush's speech after, 139
Dubai and, 12–14, 132
economic consequences of, 13–14,
62–64
GDP, post, 63
hijackers of, 34, 62, 121, 130–31,
132
ideology behind, 60–62
income decline after, 64
Intel *v.* conspiracy theories of, 33
in Islamic finance, post, 18–20
jihad and, 69–70

London, post, 97
money laundering regulations,
post, 75
Pearl Harbor and, 33
prevention of, 32, 33
shell states and, 66–67
symbolism of, 61–62
trial, xiv
violence, post, 115–16
warnings about, 34
Nixon, Richard, 81, 84
Nurbakan, Mohsen, 52

Obama, Barack, xiii, xvi, xix, 1, 137
America's new rhetoric of, 71
oil, 100
contract, long-term, 88
embargo, 84
futures market, 87–88
imported, 68
pipelines, attacks on, 88
prices, 83–84, 86–87
revenues, 47–48
supply and demand, 84
in United Arab Emirates, discovery of, 13
as a weapon, 84–86
oligarchy, 47, 51, 60
alliance between West and Muslim, 47
economic gap between masses
and, 54
Omar, Mullah, xi–xii
Omar, Omar Abu, 55
OPEC. *See* Organization of the Petroleum Exporting Countries
opium, 69
Organization of the Petroleum Exporting Countries (OPEC), 84
Saudi Arabia's role in, 86

Pakistan, xi
Palestine Liberation Organization
(PLO), 65
Palm Jumeirah, 12
Patriot Act, 12, 14, 18
acronym of, 75
banks *v.*, 76
Caribbean tax havens *v.*, 99
Colombian drug cartels *v.*, 78

debt *v.*, 74–75
dollar value *v.*, 62
European economy *v.*, 77
financial segment of, 75–76
Greenspan response to, 74–75
monetary controls of, 93–94
money laundering *v.*, 75–76
monitoring of dollar transactions,
    75–76, 78, 99–100
US economy *v.*, 76–77
Pax Britannica, 46
Pax Romana, 43
Pearl Harbor, 9/11 and, 33
pearl trading, 13
Pentagon, annual budget of, 80
PLO. *See* Palestine Liberation Organi-
    zation
policy. *See also* foreign policy
financial, 148
taxation, 4
politicians, 8, 120
deceit of, 111
strategy of fear, 111–12
politics. *See also* propaganda
of fear, 119
modern, 117
tribal, 139
Pope Urban II, 45, 54, 55
private schools, credit crunch *v.* enroll-
    ment in, 94
products
American, 137–38
fake financial, 141
sharia-compliant, 18, 19
Project for the New American Cen-
    tury, 32
propaganda, 7, 22, 39–40, 83–84
al-Qaeda's power amplified by, 61,
    64–65, 86, 109
anti-US, 90
beheading videos as, 57–58
of bin Laden, 37, 85
for children, 113
of fear, 111–13
hostages as, 58
Internet, 113, 120
of Iraqi president, 114
in media, 120
political, 70, 85
public executions as, 59

protectionism, xiii, 5–6, 135–36, 140
nationalism *v.*, 136–37
philosophy of, 137–38
public opinion, politicians manipula-
    tion of, 111–12
Putin, Vladimir, 100

al-Qaeda, xix, 14, 37, 69
finances of, 65
ideology of, 69–70
ignorance about, 59–60
in Las Vegas, 121
pre 9/11, 119
propaganda about, 61, 64–65, 86,
    109
reconnaissance videos of, 61
in Saudi Arabia, 85
strategy of, 60–62
suicide bombers of, 34
trials for members of, xvi
violence creed of, 130
Quetta, 69
Qur'an, interest prohibition of, 14–15,
    16
Qutb, Sayyid, 130

racism, 140
Ramsay, Gordon, 96
RAND Corporation, xviii
real estate, 151
boom of, 105–6
bubble, 121–22
of Dubai, 122, 123, 124, 126
interest rates *v.*, 106–7
of Las Vegas, 122–24, 126
London crash in, 101
losses, 142
over development of, 146
wealth *v.*, 145–46
rebel, right to, 8
Rebuilding America's Defenses, 32
recession. *See* economy
religion. *See also* Christianity; cru-
    sades; Islam
finance *v.*, 15–16
as identity, 53–56
laws of, 16–17, 60
reserve currency, 74
riba, 14–15, 20
Ricardo, David, 136

Rice, Condoleeza, 34
Right Went Wrong (Buchanan), 80
risk, 15–16, 149. *See also* credit; mortgages
public *v.* private, 142–43
trading of, 141, 144, 146
rollover, 91–92
Roman Empire
fall of, 43, 53
feudal system of post, 43–44
Roosevelt, Franklin Delano, 135, 152
Rudolph of Caen, 58
Rumsfeld, Donald, 32
Russians, 126
superrich, 98

Sadr city, 66
Saladin, 42, 56
Saudi Arabia, 6, 13, 62, 83
attacks on, 87
bin Laden's fatwa for, 86
bin Laden's return to, 35
al-Qaeda in, 85
role in OPEC, 86
United States and, 38
secrecy, cooperation *v.*, 28–29
seignorage, 74
sharia, 14, 60
bank compliance with, 16, 18, 19
scholars, 15
shell state(s), 68
9/11 and, 66–67
of Afghanistan, 66
definition of, 65
environments of, 66
Siegel, Bugsy, 128
simpletons, arrogance of, 109–10
slaughter, 58
Smith, Adam, 17, 135, 136, 145
Smoot-Hawley Tariff Act, 137
smuggling, 68, 69
of Congolese gold, 124–25
socialism, nationalization *v.*, 148
Soviet Union, 112
breakup of, xvi, xix, 36
collapse of, 49
jihad, anti, xvi–xvii, 35, 54, 57
starvation, 90–92
state, citizens *v.*, 4
Stiglitz, Joseph, 63

stock market, 143
crash, 96
crash of Asian, 17
losses of, 142
Sudan, 36
suicide. *See also* jihad
bombers, 34
Nevada rates of, 126
sukuk, 18
Malaysian issued, 19
superrich, 99–101
of bank sector, 107
globalization's, 12, 93–94, 95, 97
lifestyle of, 94–96
Russian, 98
Swiss Federal Bank, review of Bank al-
Taqwa, 25
symbols
of 9/11, 61–62
jihadist, 58–60
targets of Western capitalism as,
70
war against, 57–58
Syria, 84

Taliban, xi, xvii, 12
drug business of, 69
taxation
evasion of, 98, 100
laws of England, 97–99
legislation, Russian, 100
policy, 4
United Arab Emirates and, 13
tax haven(s), 73, 75
Caribbean, 99
Dubai as, 122, 124
Islamic, 22
London as, 97–99
regulation of, 77–78
taxpayers, 5
terror, new economy of, 64–71, 73–75
terrorism, xi. *See also* 9/11
9/11 as blueprint for future, 69–
70
credit crunch *v.*, 14
death penalty *v.*, xv
declining costs of, 69
definition of, xv–xvi
economy *v.*, xiii, xvi, 3, 131
fear of, 2–3, 87–88, 114, 115–19, 135

financing, 23, 27–28, 67, 68–69, 77–78
industry of, 119–20
internalization of, 117–18
justification of, 42
lexicon of, 139
meaning of, 31
MIPT-RAND data on, 115–16
mythology of, 119
national security *v.*, xiv–xv, 31
oil prices *v.*, 84–85
threat of, 2, 83–85
warnings to US about, 34
terror lists, 27–28
Nada on, 28
Thomas's, 94
throat slitting, 57–58
Time, 129
torture, 58
tourism, 125
Dubai, 122
Las Vegas, 122
toxic assets, 143
trade, 50
deficit, US, 89
flow of, 47
gold, 124–25
Treasury, US, 4–5
treasury bonds, 76–77
debt from, 4
tribalism, 139–40
Turki, Prince, 85
Turkish Islamic Development Bank (IDB), 51–52

ummah, 15–16
unemployment, xi, xiii, 63–64, 124, 125, 126, 137
in Dubai, 127
of Great Depression, 150–51
United Arab Emirates
economy of, 13
as Florida of the East, 124
gold trade of, 124–25
oil discovery in, 13
tax haven of, 13
United Self-Defense Forces of Colombia (AUC), 78
United States (US). *See also* Patriot Act
bankruptcy of, 81

budget surplus of, 1
debt of, xix, 1, 4, 39, 80, 108
dependence on China, xiii
economic model of, 144–47
economy of, 6
employment loss in, 63–64
gambling in, 122–23
gasoline prices, 64
Obama's new rhetoric for, 71
post 9/11 GDP of, 63
power of Congress in, 71
responsibility to world economy, 138
Saudi Arabia and, 38
seignorage of, 74
terrorist attack warnings to, 34
trade deficit, 89
USS Cole, 37
Uzbekistan, 49

Vaduz, 28–29
Vietnam, 2
economic consequences of, 80–81
war on terror *v.*, 80
violence, 139
political, xiv
post 9/11, 115–16
al-Qaeda's creed of violence, 130

Wahhabi, 36, 52
Wall Street, 8
Wall Street, 124
war(s)
Afghanistan, xvii, xix, 2, 39, 61
Cold, xvi, xviii, 34–35, 65, 110–15
consequences of, 116
of economic liberation, 41–43
funding of, 1–2, 5, 70–71, 71
Gulf, 35, 86
II, World, 138
Iraq, xi, xix, 2, 39, 84, 85, 114, 116
nuclear, 112–14
religious, 55
rising costs of, 70–71
against symbols, 57–58
Vietnam, 2, 80–81
of Western Europe, 44–45
of Yom Kippur, 84
war on terror, xiv–xv, xix, 3, 5, 7, 13, 22–23, 31, 56, 138

Chinese financing of, 89
cost-benefit analysis of, 70
credit crunch *v.*, 34
death toll of, 67
economic consequences of, 60–63,
    79–81
language of, 139
motives of, 29
Vietnam *v.*, 80
Waziristan, xi–xii, xvii, 66
wealth
    contraction, government *v.*, 136
    real estate *v.*, 145–46
weapons of mass destruction (WMD),
    111, 114
    Hussein *v.*, 68, 111, 136
Weimar Republic, 140
Weldon, Fay, 96
Western society, values of, 132
Wilson, Harold, 98
The Wizard of Oz, 135
WMD. *See* weapons of mass
    destruction
Wolfe, Tom, 92
Wolfowitz, Paul, 32
Woods, Grant, 97, 98–99
World War II, xviii, 138, 140, 145, 147

xenophobia, 140

Yanbu, attack on, 87
Yom Kippur, 84
yuan, dollar *v.*, 89
Yukos Oil Company, 100

zakat, 15, 26
al-Zawahiri, Ayman, xii, 55
zibah, 57–58
Zimmerman, Peter, 114

ABOUT THE AUTHOR

Loretta Napoleoni is the best-selling author of *Terror Incorporated* and *Insurgent Iraq*. She is an expert on financing of terrorism and advises several governments on counterterrorism. As chair of the countering terrorism financing group for the Club de Madrid, Napoleoni brought together heads of state from around the world to create a new strategy for combating the financing of terror networks.

Born and raised in Rome, in the mid 1970s Loretta Napoleoni became an active member of the feminist movement and a political activist. She was a Fulbright Scholar at Johns Hopkins University's Paul H. Nitze School of Advanced International Studies in Washington, DC, and a Rotary Scholar at the London School of Economics. As an economist she worked for several banks and international organizations in Europe and the US. In the early 1980s, she worked at the National Bank of Hungary on the convertibility of the forint that became the blueprint for the convertibility of the ruble a decade later.

Ms. Napoleoni is also a journalist and has worked as a foreign correspondent for several Italian financial papers. Her work appears regularly in many journals and publications, including several European newspapers. She lectures regularly on the financing of terrorism. She has written novels, guide books in Italian, and translated and edited books on terrorism; her most recent novel, *Dossier Baghdad*, is a financial thriller set during the Gulf War. She was among the few people to interview the Red Brigades in Italy after three decades of silence.

Loretta Napoleoni lives in London and Whitefish, MT, with her husband and their children.

ABOUT SEVEN STORIES PRESS

Seven Stories Press is an independent book publisher based in New York City, with distribution throughout the United States, Canada, England, and Australia. We publish works of the imagination by such writers as Nelson Algren, Russell Banks, Octavia E. Butler, Ani DiFranco, Assia Djebar, Ariel Dorfman, Coco Fusco, Barry Gifford, Hwang Sok-yong, Lee Stringer, and Kurt Vonnegut, to name a few, together with political titles by voices of conscience, including the Boston Women's Health Collective, Noam Chomsky, Angela Y. Davis, Human Rights Watch, Derrick Jensen, Ralph Nader, Loretta Napoleoni, Gary Null, Project Censored, Barbara Seaman, Alice Walker, Gary Webb, and Howard Zinn, among many others. Seven Stories Press believes publishers have a special responsibility to defend free speech and human rights, and to celebrate the gifts of the human imagination, wherever we can. For additional information, visit www.sevenstories.com.